AT THE HELM

AT THE HELM:

THE YOUNG WIDOW'S JOURNEY FROM STRUGGLE TO STRENGTH

BY AUDRA O'NEIL

NEW DEGREE PRESS

AT THE HELM

The Young Widow's Journey from Struggle to Strength

ISBN 978-1-63676-728-4 *Paperback*
978-1-63730-039-8 *Kindle Ebook*
978-1-63730-141-8 *Ebook*

TABLE OF CONTENTS

AUTHOR'S NOTE

The names of several women in this book have been changed to respect their privacy.

To Chad O'Neil, my guardian angel.

You continue to inspire me in death as you did in life.

How could he leave me here alone?
We'd been best friends for twenty years.
Our twin boys just celebrated their seventh birthday that week.
I had begged him the day before, "I can't do this without you."
Could this actually be our reality?

All I wanted was for him to open his eyes, to inhale, for the warmth to return to his cold body.

INTRODUCTION

It was the morning following Thanksgiving when my husband, Chad Mortimer O'Neil, took his final breath. He was thirty-nine years young. After five chaotic months of battling a rare demon named multiple myeloma, his breath went still.

And so, did my world.

Multiple myeloma is a cancer of the plasma cells which accumulate in the bone marrow and crowd out healthy blood cells. In short, it can cause not only kidney, heart, and other organ failure, but also pain. Older patients often live for years managing it. However, in younger people whose cells multiply more rapidly, and those with genetic mutations like Chad had, it's a death sentence.

At the end of May 2015, Chad and I traveled to Palm Desert, California. Chad had a speaking engagement for his work at Marriott, and he asked me to tag along. The entire time we were there, Chad had a sharp pain in his right hip, which was causing him to limp occasionally. As we hiked through the desert trails, took in massages at the hotel spa, or sat down for dinners on the Palm Desert Marriott's patio, the pain was front and center in our conversations. He'd had a double hernia surgery that year, coupled with an infection at the same site just months earlier, so it seemed to be the likely culprit at the time.

When we arrived home, however, Chad began experiencing an irregular increase in his heart rate known as tachycardia. His heart would race as if he were running a marathon when he was relaxed at home or in a meeting at work. His primary care physician referred him to a cardiologist, but he couldn't get an appointment for weeks. So, she sent him for an MRI, which was only one week away.

Finding out what was wrong was anything but seamless. There were incorrect scripts involved and a trip to the ER that Chad drove himself to and was sent home from because "all was well," according to them. The day after his ER visit, he was still feeling off, and he finally found a cardiologist who could see him immediately. It was a warm, sunny day, the kind of day in early June where it is summer in the sun and still winter in the shade. It must have been a Friday because I normally worked at our sons' elementary school down the road, but Fridays I had off. I was running from the grocery store to pick up our son who was sick in the school nurse's office. I had just hung up with the school when another call came in.

"Sooo...," Chad said, his voice sounding small and distant. "They say I either have a blood clot or cancer."

"What?" The hospital had just sent him home with a clean bill of health not even twelve hours earlier. "What?" I repeated. I was numb. I couldn't make sense of what he was saying.

"The doctor won't let me drive. I need you to come and pick me up."

Blur. It was all a blur. Like those TV shows where the criminal covers the victim's mouth and nose with a chloroform-drenched cloth, and everything gets fuzzy then goes black. She awakens in a different location and has no idea how she got there. That is my memory in retrospect. Somehow that day I brought Chad to the hospital, picked up our son from the nurse, asked my friend Jenn to stay with the boys while I met Chad at the hospital again, stayed for a while, and I then left him there as they prepared a room so that they could keep him for monitoring and testing.

He called later that night from the hospital room where he sat alone. "They found a tumor on my bone."

Those seven words still play like a broken record in my mind.

The guilt that I was not there with him when the doctors shared that news still haunts me.

From that moment on, the blur was endless. It was one doctor to the next. One hospital to the next. One drug to the next. Heart not pumping correctly, swollen legs, kidney failure, dialysis, port, chemo. I learned words I had never heard before and I will never forget–amyloid, light chains, platelets, Lasix, palliative care, hospice.

Five months of our lives turned upside down and inside out in hopes of one day getting Chad to a place of remission and treatment...

We never got to that place. He never had a triumph or a breakthrough. His body eventually gave out in that hopeless battle where, for young people with multiple myeloma, the cancer almost always wins.

But Chad was so much more than that disease.

Chad was a loyal friend, a loving son, a caring brother, and a dedicated husband and father. He was smart and successful, but he never took himself too seriously. He was quick to share a smile or his contagious belly laugh. Chad was one of those people who truly loved life.

During his time working for Marriott, he worked on improving a training program for front office managers. The program existed before Chad got his hands on it, but when he was finished revising it, everyone wanted to be a part. It was called "At the Helm" because it was designed to teach associates how to steer the course of the hotel's front office in a steady and positive direction.

Back in the day, when Chad was a front office manager himself, he had taken his employees out on a sailboat and was allowed by the captain to act as helmsman. Someone snapped a photograph of this, and from the moment he developed that film (yes, I said film) it was his favorite picture.

Everywhere we moved, it moved with him. It always hung in a place of honor in his home office. That photo encompassed the level of trust all his passengers held in him. The crushing weight of knowing that at any moment, by the slip of his hand, the change of wind direction, the rotation of the wheel, he could steer them off course into catastrophe or into the great beyond filled with endless possibilities.

The breeze blowing through his hair.
The freedom.
The responsibility.
The awareness of something bigger than himself.

As I muddled through the first month following Chad's death, I felt that same weight. All I could see were friends and family with healthy husbands and wives. There were, however, three women who I took solace in for different reasons:

1. My Aunt Barb, who had lost her husband a few years prior. I found out she had recently begun dating, which gave me hope that someday I may be able to picture someone else in my life.

2. My sister-in-law's mother, Karla, who had recently lost her husband. As she spoke to me of the healing she had experienced within a grief group, I realized that healing was certainly possible, although it seemed unattainable to me at the time.

3. Charity Yanishak DeNeal, a close friend whose husband, Drew, had passed away a couple years previously from

brain cancer. I saw her as a role model whose journey gave me somewhat of a future path.

While I took great comfort in our shared experience, all three of our individual experiences were very different. I know everyone has to take these steps alone, no matter how many well-meaning people are there to prop us up as we stumble and half-drown, but it would have been easier for me if there were someone I could truly relate to as a young widow while I made those steps.

I wanted—no, I *needed* answers to my rawest questions:

- Do other young widows only picture their husbands sick?
- Do they never want to wash his pillowcase because it is the only thing left that will ever smell like him again?
- Do they feel their hearts physically breaking when they hear their child cry for his father?

If only I could have found someone's story more similar to mine to help guide me through the storm when Chad died. Books had always helped me overcome challenges in my life. As my friend, Heather Hofmann, who lost her husband, Ralf, to liver, lung, and bone cancer two years ago, has said; "There is a strange comfort gained from reading other widows' stories and a confidence that I *will* get through this. So many of us feel like we are in this alone. I wish I had something to help me not only know that I wasn't alone, but also to know I would come out on the other side okay."

I can't tell you how long it was after Chad died that I walked into our local Barnes & Noble. Time was not like it is now. It was all slow motion. I can't grasp a timeline of how anything happened in those first months, but I distinctly remember the section labeled "Self-Help." My first thought was that the section itself looked sparse. Surely more people needed to help themselves than was demonstrated by this skimpy bookcase.

On one of the shelves, I found a few stories of widows, but again, none of them were my age. Older widows seemed to have similar emotions to my own, but their lives did not mirror mine closely enough for me to relate. I had young children and hope for many years ahead. I had only lived thirty-nine years. I hoped to have at least another thirty-nine ahead of me.

Books by psychologists who spoke in sterile lists about the patterns they saw in their patients peppered the shelves. Autobiographies and biographies existed telling stories of famous widows, like Veuve Clicquot, the illustrious French champagne house widow. Empowering, yes, but not what I needed at the moment (I would read them later and learn quite a bit from each one). I needed a book that spoke my language, spoke as a friend, spoke as me.

I never found that book. That one that was a careful balance between stories of real-life widows, research, and practicality. The one written from the heart about the things that young widows in particular worry about, feel, and do after the life they know falls apart. They are now at the helm and need to keep their ship afloat, solo. Even after five years of searching and reading a variety of helpful blogs, podcasts, and books, I have never found that one. So, I wrote it.

SECTION I.

CHARTING THE COURSE

"Grief is like the ocean; it comes on waves ebbing and flowing. Sometimes the water is calm, and sometimes it is overwhelming. All we can do is learn to swim."

~VICKI HARRISON, *DRESSED TO THRILL*

CHAPTER 1

THE CULTURE OF WIDOWHOOD

The trials of widows are ageless.

We can rewind all the way back to the *Book of Ruth* in the Old Testament. The story goes like this:

Naomi was married to Elimelech who died, leaving her a widow, along with two sons and two daughter in-laws. Shortly after, their two sons died, leaving behind their young widows.

One of the widows, Ruth, stuck by her mother-in-law, Naomi, and moved back to Naomi's native land. For years, these two widowed women lived in poverty, eating off the land from the field where they worked. This land belonged to a man named Boaz who happened to be distantly related to Naomi. In order for Boaz to be able to gift the land to the women, the law required Boaz to marry one of them so that heirs to the land could be conceived. Ruth married Boaz, and thanks to this coupling, both Ruth and Naomi's lives improved greatly.[1]

Throughout much of European and American history, widows have endured difficult situations—especially elderly widows and mothers of small children. These women often lived in poverty. When their husbands died, they had no trade to fall back on and no way to support themselves. Oftentimes, other male family members were named guardians to a widow's children and to her late husband's wealth.[2] The widow had no voice. According to Carolyn James in her book, *The Gospel of Ruth*, the word "widow" itself actually has Hebrew origins stemming from the word "alem," meaning "unable to speak."[3]

The historical wrongdoings toward widows were many, and to this day a number of primitive barbaric practices and inequities continue, mostly in developing countries. In many third world countries, widows have no economic or inheritance rights and are dependent upon their husband's relatives for charity. However, many times the relatives disown the widows, and they are left with nothing. Aside from poverty, in a number of countries the traditions of the people call for dangerous and repulsive actions. Parts of Africa and Asia have customary mourning rites that involve sexual relations with male relatives, scarring the widow's body, and drinking of the water that her late husband's dead body was bathed in.

1 Jack Zavada, "Introduction to the Book of Ruth."

2 *Encyclopedia.com*, s.v. "Widows and Widowers."

3 "Origin of the Word 'Widow.'"

In countries like India, widows and their daughters may be forced to beg and work in prostitution.[4]

Thankfully, there are organizations, including the Loomba Foundation and the United Nations, who work to protect and educate women in third world nations so that the death of a spouse does not destroy them. The UN has its own subagency called UN Women that focuses primarily on women's issues. Their commitment lies in areas such as ending this sort of violence against women and empowering them economically so they can make enough wages to have choices when a spouse dies. They rally governments to change national laws in order to promote gender equality.[5]

Widowers (men who have lost a spouse) do not typically pose as much of a social issue as their female counterparts. Widows outnumber widowers 11:2, according to the 2010 US Census. One reason is because men tend to die earlier than women.[6] The abundance of single women is one of the reasons why widowers are ten times more likely to remarry than widows, causing them to resign their widower status. This disproportionate remarriage rate between the sexes happens for a number of other reasons as well, one being that widowers tend to have less of a friend and support base. Also, according to Florence Isaacs in her *Legacy Connect* blog, "Widowers felt deprived by the loss of married life. But most widows appreciated the chance to be 'selfish' and focus on their own wants and needs now that they were on their own.

4 "Invisible Women, Invisible Problems."

5 Ibid.

6 Henderson, "Five Surprising Facts About Widowhood."

They were unwilling to swap these benefits for companionship plus the possibility of becoming caretakers later on."[7]

I do not specifically address widowers in this book as they have their own set of issues that another book entirely could focus upon. Nevertheless, the majority of topics discussed here absolutely apply to men who have lost a spouse. But each and every *widow* has her own set of circumstances that I cannot and do not fully understand. Some women's husbands were murdered. Some took their own lives. Some women were no longer with their husbands because they couldn't stand watching them poison themselves with drugs. These types of deaths present their own complexities. The waters for some are choppier than for others.

Despite the fact that everyone has her own story and her own grief, there are patterns that seem to emerge. Most young widows can relate to the financial difficulties that the death of a spouse often brings and, of course, to the emotional pain. We may relate to the feeling of otherness brought upon us by no longer being part of a couple.

Many young widows like myself in the United States and other developed nations are blessed with jobs and autonomy. Our children are educated regardless of our economic status, and our governments have laws preventing us from being financially divested or abused. However, this does not change the fact that we are still in a position of feeling fearful, powerless, and anxious. We have to learn things that we never had to know before. We are suddenly single. We have to reinvent

---

7 Florence Isaacs, "Why More Widowers Date, Remarry Than Widows."

ourselves and our lives in order to live in this coupled world, despite our lack of experience going it alone.

I have been on this journey, at the helm, for five years now. I have spent the past three years researching the topic of young widows, as well as grief and hope. I still have so much to learn, but I also have so much to share. I have read about, listened to, and interviewed young widows in an attempt to learn everything I could to help myself and eventually to help others.

I have been fortunate enough to have met many young widows in my community, through friends, and online. These women's stories are some you will hear throughout the pages of this book. My hope is that you find them relevant to your own life as a young widow. I hope you are able to use the information and stories in this book to help you feel part of a larger community where your sadness is understood and your desire for joy, connection, and contentment nourished.

CHAPTER 2

THE SCIENCE OF GRIEF

There is an episode in the series *Monk* where the main character, an obsessive-compulsive widower, discovers his therapist of many years is quitting his practice. Monk is entirely reliant on this man. In one hysterical scene, he loops through the stages of grief repeatedly within the course of five minutes.

Monk starts off by thinking his therapist is joking. In a split second, he screams at him, "Damn you, Charles! Damn you to hell!" Instantly, he bargains with him. "I can hire you full time and put you on the payroll." Immediately following is depression. "Why me? Everyone is always leaving me." And in the same breath, he accepts. "I'm just going to have to find another doctor. Thanks to you, I can get past this."

As he walks away, Monk starts spiraling back through the stages again.

I am certain that no one experiences the stages of grief at this rate, but it is a comical depiction of Elisabeth Kübler-Ross's stage model. In the past, the Kübler- Ross stage model depicted above was what most experts in the field of psychology used as their map toward healing. Before my husband died in 2015, I saw a counsellor at the cancer center where he received treatments, and she told me about the stages of grief I would go through.

Each day after Chad died, and even before, I would run through the list, trying to figure out if I was feeling denial, anger, bargaining, or depression; definitely not acceptance.[8]

I wondered why one day I could be angry at everything and the next I could feel pretty normal, like it didn't happen, and I was in denial. Wasn't I supposed to move forward through these stages? Certainly not backward.

It wasn't until I decided to embark upon some grief research of my own that I came to find that these stages were first based on a study of people who were actually dying themselves. They were the stages the terminally ill passed through on their way toward the end. Kübler-Ross's initial book that introduced these stages was named *On Death and Dying*. Later, she applied these stages again to the grieving in her book coauthored by David Kessler, *On Grief and Grieving*. (I highly recommend reading this book, by the way.) Understanding that this theory first related to the dying was a huge revelation for me.[9]

Yes! Yes! Yes! When Chad was diagnosed, he experienced denial ("This will not take me, Audra") to anger ("Fuck Cancer") and bargaining ("If I beat this, I will work less"),

---

8 Elisabeth Kübler-Ross and David Kessler, *On Grief*, 7.

9 Ibid.

depression (silence), and finally, acceptance ("I'm ready to make that goodbye video for the boys now").

Even with him, the order of these seemed to flip flop. Kübler-Ross herself clearly indicated that these stages are anything but linear, as they were in the *Monk* scenario. Understanding this helped me realize I was not crazy. We are allowed to grieve in any way that suits us best, not in an organized pattern or by someone else's map. In truth, there is no "one" healthy way to grieve.

What Sigmund Freud called "grief work" back in the early 1900s was something that has been expected from those grieving for decades. I personally need to do this sort of work; to talk, cry, look at pictures, listen to sad music, and work through my memories of Chad's illness and his death. But no one should do this all the time. I did feel denial, anger, and depression. I did bargain. And little by little, I came to a place of acceptance that my husband was dying, and he would no longer be in our lives. Along the path of bereavement, I also lived long stretches happy, relieved, and content. Not every moment of a widowed person's life is spent dwelling on it.[10]

In 1999, Margaret Stroebe and Henk Schut, both renowned authors and bereavement researchers, addressed this issue when they introduced the idea of the dual process model of grief. This theory suggests that the bereaved vacillate between orientating to the loss and restoring themselves.

---

10 Elizabeth A. Doughty et al., *Current Trends in Grief Counseling*, 2.

Robert A. Neimeyer, PhD, a professor in the department of psychology at the University of Memphis and author of over thirty books about transition and grief, says that on one side of the pendulum, we need to be in contact with our grief. We have private conversations with people whom we trust about how difficult it is and how hopeless we feel.[11]

On the other side is "necessary restoration." He says, "Sometimes we need to replace foundation stones in that [old] world in order to find a new place on which to stand." While we do this, we push away grief so that we can put our energy into rebuilding ourselves. "The grief will always be available to us as a kind of room where we can knock on the door and reenter that space of grieving, or where we hear the knock and call of grief, sometimes when we least expect it." But Neimeyer believes this model demonstrates the choice we have of how and when we knock and respond. We are not at all times engaging in grief. We are in control and rebuilding and strengthening ourselves as well.[12]

George Bonanno, a professor of clinical psychology at Columbia University and renowned researcher in the field of bereavement and trauma, believes that "for most of us, grief is not overwhelming or unending. As frightening as the pain of loss can be, the most common trajectory we've seen among bereaved people is the trajectory of resilience."[13]

---

11 Robert Neimeyer, "The Dual Process Model," 2:23-5:59.

12 Ibid.

13 George Bonanno, *The Other Side*, 16:08.

He recognizes that in our society, we think of grief as an overwhelming, never-ending process. We assume it will cast a shadow on our lives forever. He disagrees, saying, "Most bereaved people get better on their own without any kind of professional help. They may be deeply saddened. They may feel adrift for some time, but their life eventually finds its way again. Often more easily than they thought possible. This is the nature of grief. This is human nature." Some people, of course, will not find their way as easily. And those who do not will need to seek the support of a mental health professional.[14]

I absolutely agree that we are more resilient than we believe ourselves to be. I have seen it with my own eyes. Personally, my grief has lessened with time to a point where I am no longer actively grieving. However, I do not believe that grief ever completely ends.

We have all heard those terms that allude to the idea that it does. They make my skin crawl: "letting go," "moving on," "getting over it," or getting back to "the new normal." I prefer the term I learned from the *One Fit Widow* blog, by Michelle Steinke-Baumgard, "moving forward."[15] As for all the other terms, I was never normal in the first place, and with letting go and moving on, frankly, that makes me envision placing my memories and years with Chad in a cardboard box, taping it tightly shut, and walking away forever. That is not how this works.

---

14 Bonanno, *The Other Side*, 1:00:59.

15 Michelle Steinke-Baumgard, *Healthy Living: A Guide to Working Out Grief*, 16.

I believe the end goal as a young widow is to be able to live a full life and grow around our grief, to move forward and experience joy once again. With these steps forward, I hope to continue to learn and become stronger. In Sheryl Sandburg and Adam Grant's book, *Option B*, they call this "post-traumatic growth." Adam Grant, a psychologist and professor at Wharton School at the University of Pennsylvania, and Sheryl Sandberg, the COO of Facebook whose husband passed away at forty-seven-years-old, came together to write this book. Their chapter about post-traumatic growth is appropriately entitled "Bouncing Forward." It gives examples of all the ways people in grief can grow *because* of their losses. Sandburg quotes Viktor Frankl, psychiatrist and Holocaust survivor, "When we are no longer able to change the situation, we are challenged to change ourselves."[16]

According to an article written in *Psychology Today*, this post-traumatic growth phenomenon was discovered in the late 1990s by psychologists Richard Tedeschi and Lawrence Calhoun. Approximately two-thirds of people who experience trauma will also experience this type of growth.

We can potentially grow in several ways. We may recognize new opportunities or improve relationships with loved ones and with others who have suffered. We may develop an inner strength from recognizing that we have been through one of the most difficult obstacles life can throw at us. We may appreciate life more.[17]

---

16 Sheryl Sandberg and Adam Grant, *Option B*, 78.

17 "Post-Traumatic Growth."

Post-traumatic growth is not just surviving, but rather growing and learning. I have heard stories of this type of post-traumatic growth, time and time again, in my conversations with young widows.

Many of the widows whom I interviewed in the following pages appreciated life more after their husbands' deaths, like my neighbor Nicki Bunting. Nicki's husband, Bubba, was on tour in Afghanistan in the gulf of Kandahar when his armed convoy hit a pressure mounted IED. The blast killed everyone inside—four American soldiers, including Bubba, and their Afghan interpreter. "I have learned and try to teach my boys that there is so much good in the world, and we need to be grateful. Some people live their lives almost with a chip on their shoulder, and they are miserable. It is so much better to be happy."

My coworker and friend Lacey Bruno's spirituality was affected. When I met with Lacey last spring, she arrived with a picture of her husband, Pat, that she propped up on the outdoor table at Starbucks. Pat was a handsome young Irish man with an opioid addiction. At thirty-eight he overdosed and died. "No matter what, this world is always going to look at his death as a bad thing. 'What a horrible thing that he was an IV drug user. He lost his job, his wife, his son, his sense of value, his self-worth.' But God meant it all for good. It made me a better person, a more compassionate person, a better Christian, and it made my son a better person too."

Andrea Albanese, whom I met through a mutual friend when her husband died of the same cancer as Chad's at the age of forty-two, has five children. She has come so far in finding her inner strength. "The biggest thing I have learned through trauma is competence. I now have that assurance that I could do anything if I had to. I've healed in a lot of ways from losing Jim. I had a lot of anger in the beginning from being forced to handle the stuff he did and I took for granted: financials, rentals, IEPs, back-up disciplinarian.... Now I know I can do it because I've done it."

I asked Charity Yanishak DeNeal, a longtime friend from college whose husband Drew, one of Chad's closest friends, died from a brain tumor at age thirty-seven, if she ever looked at grief as a gift. Her initial reaction was to laugh. "No! I had a great marriage and a great guy. I have that again and I'm very lucky." She added, as her voice broke, "But I would have him back in a second." Despite this perspective, she did attest to post-traumatic growth. "We don't know what is going to happen in life, but if I were my older self, telling my younger self, I would say, 'Don't give yourself such a hard time.' Having loss in our thirties, we are at a place that most people don't get to until they are in their fifties. You learn that you can't compare yourself to another woman. *Your* journey is *your* journey. It will never be the same as someone else's."

I am a collector of words and quotes. My Pinterest boards are filled with them. So many authors and thinkers have touched upon this very idea of strength gained through struggle. Here are a few quotes that have motivated me over the past few years:

"I may not have gone where I intended to go, but I think I've ended up where I needed to be." —Douglas Adams

"She understood that the hardest times in life to go through were when you were transitioning from one version of yourself to another." —Unknown

"I can't go back to yesterday because I was a different person." —C.S. Lewis

"I do not understand the mystery of grace, only that it meets us where we are but does not leave us where we found it." —Anne Lamot

"Adversity introduces a man to himself." —Albert Einstein

"The Universe buries strange jewels inside of all of us and then stands back to see if we can find them." —Elizabeth Gilbert

"The scars of tragedy become the birth of wisdom." —Miriam Neff

"No man ever steps in the same river twice, for it's not the same river and he's not the same man." —Heraclitus

In a *TED Talk* given by psychologist and writer Dr. Geoff Wharburton, he noted that we all will likely be in an "emotional abyss" after loss. He says:

> *You may feel that, in that abyss, a part of you is dying. And maybe a part of you needs to die. Close off your experience of the abyss, then you close off the flow of life. Block that anger and you block your vitality. Block that fear and you block your excitement. Block that deep emotional pain and you block your access to compassion. Even block*

> *your hatred and you block your access to peace. Block your experience to that abyss, and you will block access to who you really are and the energy that's going to take you forward.*[18]

If we allow ourselves to dive into the abyss, as messy as it may be; if we embrace every wave of every feeling that may flood over us, like sea glass, the tumultuous current may just place us back on land with softened edges that mirror our newfound wisdom and growth.

---

18 Geoff Warburton, "The Adventures of Grief."

SECTION II.

TURBULENCE

"Your struggles don't mean you are weak, they mean you are human."

—RACHEL HOLLIS, *GIRL, STOP APOLOGIZING*

CHAPTER 3

MAKING A PLACE FOR HIM

"I want to be where you and the boys are."

A dying man's seemingly straightforward answer to the unimaginable question of where he wanted the remains of his body to go when his heart stopped beating.

I was lying on Chad's hospital bed in the cancer unit at Johns Hopkins Hospital in Baltimore, Maryland. Chad lay next to me with leads guiding the chemotherapy poison into his bloodstream. With heart monitor's blinking and beeping, a tan and olive crocheted prayer shawl draped around his frail shoulders, his teeth yellow from all the drugs he had taken in the fight to get well, his thirty-nine-year-old body had transformed into that of a ninety-three-year-old man. I knew we did not have long. I needed to know the details. I needed him to have at least some say in what came next. He had been robbed of all choices. This one belonged only to him.

The doctors had just left the room having informed us that, after a brave battle, the cancer had spread throughout his body. The evil dark cancer cells had finally usurped the friendly ones. With complete certainty, the doctors looked Chad in the eye, and they told him he did not have long; they had never seen such an aggressive form of multiple myeloma.

As the door shut quietly behind them, I laid my head on Chad's arm (the chemo port on his chest making it awkward to place it in my usual spot) and began to sob. In his best attempt to comfort me, Chad's weary voice said, as he always said, "This will not take me."

But this time, he knew that it would.

In the months leading up to this moment, I had tried rather gingerly to determine Chad's last wishes. Because he despised the topic, he refused to think that he would one day have to give up the fight.

Gradually, I drew out reluctant answers.

"What do *you* want to happen to you when *you* die?" he asked. I told him about my irrational fear of waking up in a casket underneath the earth like I had seen in an Alfred Hitchcock television show when I was a child. I'm a bit claustrophobic. I definitely preferred cremation. "Then I want to be cremated too," he agreed.

When I asked where he would want his ashes to go, he already seemed to have determined that he wanted them to be placed somewhere specific, not spread in multiple locations as some people preferred.

At the end, he was clear about where he wanted them to be.

The problem was that this wish was not easy to grant. When Chad died five days later, the very last thing I knew was what came next for me and our children. I had no clear vision of where I would be tomorrow, let alone where I would be in a year.

Initially, no one spoke of the white marble urn embossed with gold cursive letters that sat in the sanctuary of the church at his funeral, the same urn that resided beside my bed a year afterward. One day, when a few of Chad's college friends were visiting, one of them, Egan, approached me with something that was bothering him.

"Andy and I were talking, and we feel like we don't really have closure because Chad wasn't buried."

Huh? That thought had never crossed my mind. I had just gone with my gut and planned in a way that felt natural to me. I never really took other's beliefs into account. Egan is Catholic, and most of his experience with death involved a casket and a headstone. I knew that Chad wanted to be cremated, but I didn't know what to do with him next. It was as simple as that.

That conversation with Egan was a catalyst for me. I decided to find a place to lay Chad to rest. The boys and I, after exploring a number of beautiful and serene options, found the perfect historical garden cemetery by a river in Georgetown, DC. I had a beautiful stone carved for Chad with an old Irish saying encircling his name and a Celtic cross:

May the road rise up to meet you.
May the wind be always at your back.
May the sun shine warm upon your face;
the rains fall soft upon your fields
And until we meet again,
May God hold you in the palm of His hand.

We had a small ceremony with close friends and family in the circular stone columbarium where the urn would remain forevermore.

In retrospect, I'm glad that Egan propelled me to make this decision. After all, we now have a physical place to visit Chad, just as he had wished, near us. However, after five years of reflection, and a gained knowledge and wisdom that only time and experience bring, I recognize that all that pomp and circumstance of the interment ceremony may not have been in the name of my top two priorities: me and my boys. I initially did it because I thought I was supposed to. Nevertheless, Chad would have loved the place we chose. Knowing that I did right by him comforts me.

Laura Keller, a friend who I met through a hospice grief group that we attended together after our husbands died, had a similar dilemma. In 2009, her husband Joe was a healthy and happy forty-four-year-old. As time progressed, Joe started having stomach ailments and other pains. Over time, he went to the doctor and the ER repeatedly, and all found nothing wrong with him. By 2010, Joe's pain was getting worse. He was diagnosed with Stage 4 pancreatic cancer that had metastasized to his liver. They gave him two to five years. He lived five years and one month.

Laura and her eleven-, thirteen-, and fifteen-year-old children were left without a husband and father. "He never discussed what he wanted, which was not helpful," Laura said. She had to decide whether to bury or cremate him. She eventually decided upon cremation. After a few days, the morgue delivered his ashes to her in a small fabric sack resembling a lunch bag with the name of the funeral parlor on it. Not having planned with Joe what to do with his ashes, the lunch bag stayed in her closet for years. "I would say, 'Hi, Joe,' when I would walk into the closet," Laura remembers.

She realized a few years in that this was not what she wanted Joe's fate to be. She remembered as a younger woman visiting Joe's parents and seeing the remains of their cat displayed in their home. "I thought, that is so weird and creepy, why would someone do that? Then, I have my dead husband in my closet!"

Four years later, the ashes in Laura's closet were the only unfinished business that the family had left. They knew they wanted Joe's remains to be in a cemetery, but no one wanted to take that step that made everything feel so final. Eventually, Laura found herself mentally ready, and she chose a cemetery. When she spoke to the director, he asked her if she would want to be there when Joe was interred. Of course, she and her daughters would be there.

Laura thought she was clear in saying that it would be only the four of them at the interment. The following week, when they showed up to the cemetery with Joe's ashes, there was a surprise waiting for them. The director had misunderstood that only the immediate family would be attending. "When we arrived, they had set up a tent, complete with fifteen plus chairs and velvet, the whole nine yards. It was terribly awkward for the four of us. And, since we weren't doing a service, we were kind of just standing around, which made it sort of terrible and sort of ridiculous all at the same time."

For most everyone who experiences the death of a loved one, what to do with the remains of the deceased is just the beginning of making a place for them and for us in this new reality. We need to figure out what to do with finances, his clothes, the belongings from his desk at work, and the boxes in storage filled with treasures from his youth.

The house becomes both a comfort and an enemy. Sometimes we can picture times of sadness in it, and sometimes we can picture times of happiness. The one place where we should feel most whole is the one place where we can't escape the flood of emotions and memories.

We could leave our homes entirely, and some do. Or we could keep them as a shrine to our lost loves, a museum with all the artifacts that prove this person once lived, but hanging on to the past is no way to move forward.

I know. I realize it is easier said than done.

The pain of letting go of material things can make us feel like we are losing our person all over again. David Kessler, psychologist, grief researcher, and author of *Finding Meaning: The Sixth Stage of Grief,* says, "Even taking practical steps like closing their bank and credit card accounts and having their phones turned off seems to make their footprint here on earth smaller."[19]

I remember finding a paper tucked away under a board in Chad's workroom in the basement. On the paper was a list of which room each fuse went to in the fuse box. I sat with this paper for an hour, examining it. It was a window into his thinking. I could glimpse a small moment of his life when he was alone and quiet. It was proof that he once thought and planned and existed. I still keep that paper in the drawer of my desk, not because I need to remember the fuse connections, but sometimes I need something tangible to help me remember *him.*

In the following sections, I delve deeper into what I did with my husband's belongings. It may be comforting to know that many widows continue to hold onto their spouse's items years after death.

Melanie Green, whom I met through a mutual friend, says, "I'm stuck there. I wear his wedding ring on my middle finger. Anytime I leave the house I always have to wear it. I have not gotten rid of anything, nothing. I'm sentimentally attached to it. I've moved things around, like I moved his socks so

---

19 David Kessler, *Finding Meaning: The Sixth Stage of Grief,* 215.

that I could have a new bra drawer, but I'm kind of cheating because I'm shuffling."

Melanie's husband, Jon, died two years ago at age forty-three from an aortic aneurysm rupture, and she is just not ready. She did end up selling his truck. One day, she took it out for a drive and the brakes didn't work. She got back home, fortunately in one piece, but this was the catalyst she needed to finally part with it. "I felt like there was a higher above person pulling some strings for me. I guess I felt like it was Jon."

Nicki Bunting, whose husband Bubba died twelve years ago, says about his belongings, "They're always in my basement cedar closet. It's stupid, but whatever. If I got rid of them, I feel like I would be getting rid of a part of him, and I'm just not ready to do that."

She had some of Bubba's T-shirts made into quilts for her two sons. "That took me, like, five years to be able to do because I pictured someone cutting into his shirts. But I eventually just took the plunge, and I'm so happy I did!" Nicki chose specific shirts for each quilt that had special meaning for each son. For instance, her son Connor's quilt has in it the shirt that Bubba wore the night that Connor was born. These quilts will always bring the boys warmth and comfort, and they are part of Bubba's legacy.

Two other items that Nicki needed to make a place for when Bubba died were his wedding band and her own. His wedding band was lost in the blast when he died. It melted off. But they had two sets of rings because they first eloped and then later had a ceremony. Nicki buried Bubba with her elopement wedding band, and she kept all the others in case her boys would like them in the future. Nicki keeps the bands in a fireproof safe because she knows firsthand that metal can burn and melt, and she is not willing to let that happen. Nicki wore her wedding band for the longest time until she just recently had a new band made that she wears on her left ring finger. "It's just a little bit different than my wedding ring, you know, but it still makes me feel married to him."

Like Nicki, I felt wrong taking off my ring too, but I did not want to wear it either. I went through a bunch of transitions before settling on something I feel comfortable with now. About a month after Chad's death, I started wearing his ring around my neck on a chain (very heavy—too heavy). Then I switched from wearing a necklace with his birthdate engraved (too many questions asked that I didn't always feel like answering) to wearing a necklace that friends gave me with the word LOVE on it.

Finally, when I was cleaning out my jewelry box, I found a diamond pendant that Chad had given to me one Christmas when we were dating. He had presented it to me with a chain around the neck of a stuffed polar bear. I remember feeling so in love when I opened the card and written on it was, "A little piece of ice for my love."

I polished the setting, purchased a new chain, and I have been wearing this for almost two years. I don't take it off. I feel like I still have a piece of Chad next to my heart, but it doesn't bring me sadness or flood me with memories that may be unwelcome.

According to the blog *Cake*, many women continue to wear their rings on their wedding ring finger. Some women wear it around their necks, some switch it to their right hand, some take it off and never wear it again. The author of the blog, Sheree McDonald, notes that "you might see moving your ring [to your right hand] as a 'baby step' toward not wearing it." It also "allows you to keep holding onto the person you love, but indicates your unmarried status," in case you may want to begin dating again one day.[20]

Each and every one of us has a different method and timeline for making a space for our spouses. No one should be rushed or advised of a "right way" to do it. It is very personal.

At some point, however, according to David Kessler, it may be healthy to let some of your spouse's things go. Kessler says, "Our belongings can become a trap when we find ourselves unable to part with them."[21] He has a clever idea of taking a photograph before getting rid of an item: Photograph, then pass on the less important items. Keep the ones most meaningful to you. [22]

Kessler lost his son when he was young, so he can relate to the importance of making a place for the items that our loved ones leave behind. He refers to these items as part of their legacy. However, it is helpful to think that we—the people they leave behind—are their greatest legacy.

---

20 "Nine Things to Do with Your Wedding Ring After a Spouse's Death."

21 Kessler, *Finding Meaning*, 215

22 Kessler, *Finding Meaning*, 217

"You are unique in all the world for having known that person. You are the living, breathing evidence that the person lived."[23]

When I look at my children, I know Kessler is correct. My son Matthew's attention to detail in his work, Connor's sense of humor—these are Chad's true legacy. And these are just some of the ripples that Chad created in life and in death. His legacy lives on well beyond our nuclear family. It is not in his watches, pens, and T-shirts. It is in the way we now live because his life was once woven into ours.

---

23 Ibid.

CHAPTER 4

THE OTHERS

"You are a combination of the five people you hang out with most."

—RACHEL HOLLIS[24]

According to Rachel Hollis, entrepreneur, blogger and author of *Girl, Wash Your Face* and *Girl, Stop Apologizing,* in order to move forward, women need to surround themselves with people who inspire them, not bring them down. Hollis's books encompass the themes of self-betterment and the ability to rise above one's current situation. In her book, *Girl, Stop Apologizing,* she urges women to stop listening to negative self-talk and the comments of others and have the courage to believe in themselves.[25]

I recognize that we should not put stock into what other's think, but I have yet to overcome that barrier in life. I would

---

24 Rachel Hollis, *Girl, Stop Apologizing: A Shame-Free Plan for Embracing and Achieving Your Goals,* 129.

25 Ibid.

love to be able to tell Rachel Hollis, "Girl, I have stopped apologizing!" But I would be lying. Even writing this book, to me, is like dancing naked in front of an open window at night while the neighbors are walking their dogs. It leaves me exposed, open to criticism, judgment, and other people's perceptions of right and wrong.

It is especially difficult for me not to imagine what my late husband's family thinks of me. There were times when Chad was sick, and even the day that he was dying, that we did not see eye to eye. Chad did not like to be alone in the hospital overnight, so my father-in-law would fly in from Texas whenever this occurred. His father would often stay in our home and commute back and forth an hour to Baltimore to be with Chad. It was the most amazing gift from father to son, and I am still grateful for that time that Chad had with his dad. Living in that stressful state, though—raising children alone, trying to manage my dying husband's care, and dealing with all of the emotions, his, mine, and our children's, trying to work, and then having my father-in-law living with us led to various strained relationships.

It is probably one of the most difficult things a person can go through in life watching her life partner slip away, or having him abruptly removed, and watching her children grieve for the father and future they will never have. On the other hand, I have never lost a child. When I even begin to think of it, I feel nauseous. Tears sting in the corners of my eyes; my heart literally aches. I cannot imagine what Chad's parents are going through, and since neither of my in-laws have gone through losing a spouse, they cannot imagine what I am going through. Without a middleman to negotiate it all, the relationship is made more difficult. In my situation, we have learned to meet halfway. They have accepted me for who I am, and I accept them for who they are. I always try to be mindful that they are hurting too and have lost a son.

Other people's judgment can and does hurt us, no matter how much we steel ourselves so it won't or tell ourselves that it shouldn't. People are generally kind, but most are not schooled in how to navigate through another's grief. The majority don't know what to say to a wife who lost her spouse too early. So, they either say nothing, or what comes out can be hurtful. I try to tell myself that people don't mean to be cruel, but they sure can be.

In Kelly Lynn's *TED talk*, "When Someone You Love Dies, There Is No Such Thing as Moving On," she tells the story of a widow who would carry a chair in her car because she sat on it when she would visit her husband's grave. One day, her friends decided that she should be getting over her grief and should not visit as often as she did. They removed the chair from her car. She tells of another man whose friends offered him money for each picture of his wife that he would take down from display in his home. Eventually, she said, these grieving people just stopped talking about their loved ones. Of course, they did not stop grieving. They just did it alone.[26]

Nicki Bunting is infuriated when mothers whose husbands coach, and therefore are not home often during the season of

---

26 Kelly Lynn, "When Someone You Love Dies, There Is No Such Thing as Moving On."

that sport, say, "I'm a wrestling widow" or "I'm a golf widow." To that, Nicki says, "SHUT UP!"

She is hurt by people comparing death to divorce. One mother asks Nicki to take her child for playdates often because she is divorced. This mother tells her, "I just can't do it. I have had them for ***four*** days." Nicki never gets a break, like most parents who have lost a spouse. She has no family in the area, and even if she did, no one could give the break that the child's other parent could have. "She's barking up the wrong tree," Nicki says about her friend.

She has coined herself a "solo" parent versus a "single" parent, a slight of phrase that I have adopted from her. Nicki's friends, like the one just mentioned, are single parents. Most get breaks, and they have someone to talk to about their child's successes, struggles, and futures; someone who cares just as much about the child as they do. Even if they may not choose to be married to that person, their child has two parents. Their children have not lived through one of the most traumatic events possible in a young person's life—the death of a parent. Single is so much different than solo.

Stacy Feintuch's husband, Howie, was forty-five when he died of a heart attack. She and a friend started a website called Living the Second Act, a community for women in their forties and fifties designed to share their life stories. Part of this website is Stacy's blog, *Widow Wears Pink*. In her blog, Stacy mentions numerous times how social media can be painful to her, her children, and other young widows. "When you are unhappy with the circumstances of your life or are going through a tragedy or just a hard time, it can be difficult to see everyone around you posting how deliriously happy they are all the time."[27]

We all know that most people only post the happy things, the pictures where they think they look good, so no one truly gets a glimpse into the real lives of Facebook friends. But, like Feintuch says, "It can make you feel very alone—like you are the only one whose life is sad or difficult." Feintuch refuses to even open Facebook on special occasions, like Father's Day. "The pictures and posts are way too hard to see."[28]

Lacey Bruno has a long-time friend who just lost her husband three months ago to the same fate as her own husband—drugs. As her friend shared the hurtful things people were saying, Lacey could remember the same things being said to her. Both women had left their husbands months before their deaths because their addictions had led them to habits that the women no longer could live with. "Well, you weren't still with him, so what is the big deal?" people would ask.

They did not move out because they did not love their husbands. They moved out because they could no longer watch their husbands kill themselves. Many people asked Lacey and her friend as well, "Are you going to change your name back?" as if their relationship never happened. It seems as if people could not relate to what these two women were experiencing, so they downplayed it and said malicious things, likely to make themselves feel better in some way. These off-the-cuff

---

27 Stacy Feintuch, "Facebook Can Be Hard."

28 Ibid.

comments have stuck with Lacey Bruno for fifteen years as the most difficult part of losing her husband.

Melanie Green, whose husband Jon died two years ago, finds the silence and lack of acknowledgment more painful than any words. She has good friends who look out for her, but there are some who offer up social outings, but they never act upon the offer. "They reach out to say they did it. It's a nicety." Many people don't know how to help, but some want to say that they did so they can check that box. They never actually follow through, but they think that they have been kind to the poor widow and done their due diligence. It would have been easier if they had never offered at all.

Teresa Snow's husband, Mark, was the buffer between her and his parents. Teresa always struggled with Mark's parents, but when he died, she had no one on her side. It was now two-against-one. Teresa's mother-in-law would criticize her about having a cleaning lady, a babysitter, even how she took care of Mark while he was sick.

Mark's dying wish was to spend his final moments in their home. His mother ignored this wish and told Teresa that was a bad idea because it would traumatize the children. Teresa tells the story of one particularly challenging day while Mark was in hospice care. Teresa had been juggling work, caring for her children, and taking care of her husband who was now bound to a hospital bed in their living room because of the progression of his cancer. Mark was difficult to care for at the time because the steroids he was taking for palliative care made him miserable, angry, and confrontational.

Mark's parents stopped over, as they only lived five minutes down the road.

Teresa went to the back porch to vent to her mother-in-law about how hard this all was. Her mother-in-law said, "Well, you know the reason I can't sleep at night?" Teresa assumed she was going to talk about her son dying. No. She said, "Because you send your son to Catholic school, and you need to simplify your life rather than complicate it." Teresa was stunned. "Instead of talking about the elephant in the room, like, hey this is really hard. My son is dying. She is upset about Catholic school."

Since Mark's passing, Teresa's father-in-law has become even more insulting. He has asked to review her taxes, contacted her accountant, financial planner, and her son's guidance counsellor for access to her son's grades without her permission. "He has a total lack of trust in me. I've said, 'You've overstepped your boundaries. Just be a grandfather.' But nothing changes."

Teresa has learned to lower her expectations of her in-laws, as her therapist coached her to do. She no longer counts on them to babysit or help with the kids. However, Teresa still wishes that they would have a relationship with them. She hears from family friends that Mark's sister visits with her children, but no one reaches out for her children to join them. Her parents, who live in Ohio, see her family more than her in-laws who live down the road. She now knows that is the reality of their situation, and she is learning to accept it.

Another widow I interviewed, Kim Chao, had similar difficulties with her in-laws. Kim lost her husband in a car accident when he was twenty-seven. Kim, like Teresa, wanted her children to have a relationship with their grandparents after her husband died. Also, like Teresa, Kim's in-laws did not come to visit her at all. They expected her to board a plane with her two very young sons and fly across the ocean to Europe each summer. Kim did as was expected each year, but the last time she visited was especially painful for her. "I know that they didn't mean to hurt me purposefully as much as they did," she says. But bottom line, they did.

Where Kim's in-laws live, it is customary to have the children outside and active all day. While Kim and the boys were there, the family took a seven-mile hike. Kim's boys were only four and six-years-old at the time. Like many young children, her boys did not have the stamina for this. To make matters worse, the boys weren't eating there because the food was so different from what they were accustomed. When exhaustion and hunger got the better of them, they turned to crying and bickering. Their grandfather yelled at them, "What is wrong with you?" Her brother-in-law said, "You boys are stupid."

Later in the visit, some of Kim's late husband's friends came over to visit. The wife took Kim aside for what seemed like an intervention. She said, "Your kids are obnoxious, and they have no manners." Kim broke down crying, and the woman said, "Oh, I know you miss him," meaning her husband. As if what she had just said about Kim's children had no bearing on why the young widow in front of her was crumbling.

I asked Kim if she would go back. I asked her why she tolerates this treatment when she is in total control of whether or not her in-laws ever see her or her children again. Kim says, "I haven't found my strength yet with other people. I can't wait to get there."

In his book, *Finding Meaning*, David Kessler says about those who constantly disappoint, "You can rail against them as you have every right to do, or you can simply accept them for who they are.... However, hoping they will be different than they are only leads to more turmoil."[29] Ultimately, we have the choice of who we surround ourselves with. We can't change others, but we can change how we react to them, and we can choose if they are present in our lives.

Sometimes the things that others say that hurt us most are actually meant to be helpful. Personally, I'm not looking to surround myself with people who tell me to "be strong," "look on the bright side," or "find the silver lining." This is what psychologists refer to as "toxic positivity." According to clinical psychologist, Konstantin Lukin, PhD, toxic positivity "refers to the concept that being only positive, and keeping positive only, is the right way to live your life. It means only focusing on positive things and rejecting anything that may trigger negative emotions."[30]

Lukin warns that trying to always put off a positive vibe actually makes those unpleasant emotions even worse. People

---

29 David Kessler, *Finding Meaning: The Sixth Stage of Grief*, 243.

30 "Toxic Positivity: Don't Always Look on the Bright Side."

who always put off that vibe seem less approachable because they appear to not have any problems.[31]

For me, I just want to be heard. I don't want to be around people who say it will all be okay. It won't always be okay. I appreciate those people who say, "Yep. This sucks." Whenever I share my feelings with my friend Jenn, she simply listens completely. She does not try to cheer me up or change my mind. Instead, she says, "Feel the feels." Clearly, she is one of my five people.

31 Ibid.

CHAPTER 5

HOLIDAYS

"Who is the big fucking liar who coined the phrase "time heals all wounds?" That's just not true. I would go so far as to argue that, when it comes to the loss of a spouse, the exact opposite might actually be true: time worsens and infects all wounds. In fact, time takes a sharp steak knife and stabs those old wounds over and over until they're bleeding again. Why? Because we widows, badass or otherwise, can't help but mark time with birthdays of our deceased spouses, death anniversaries, and other incredibly depressing date markers. So, to whomever coined that stupid phrase "time heals all wounds," shame on you for making some of us feel like we're not doing a good enough job in our healing processes." [32]

—MARY KATE TICHLER

Mary Kate Tishler, the author of the *Badass Widow* blog whose husband died of a heart attack at age forty-seven while

32 Mary Kate Tischler, "'Time Heals All Wounds:' I Call Bullshit!"

at the dog park, speaks her truth about how many widows feel, at one point or another, in relation to the holidays.[33]

We may be going about our business, thinking that we have come so far, having fewer, less painful episodes of grief, and then October rolls around. On the Facebook groups for young widows and widowers that I belong to, the majority of the posts veer toward dread of the holidays and anticipational grief in October. We worry about what's to come. Can we handle all the emotions and memories? Can we tolerate all the blatant joy and happiness surrounding us? Will we be able to fake our enjoyment well enough to convince our children that all is well with the world?

Stacy Feintuch describes holidays as "a time when his absence almost screamed at me." The missing chair at the table; the void of what could and should have been, had he been there. She tells the story of how she watched a *Shark Tank* marathon one New Year's Eve, just so she didn't have to experience midnight.[34] The changing of another year. Another year that her husband would miss. Another year without him.

Nicki Bunting says, "All of our Christmases and our birthdays and all of our happy occasions are not 100 percent happy anymore. I try so hard to make my kids happy and put the smile on, but there's simply a piece of me that is just like, 'This isn't right. He should be here. He should be smiling.' And that doesn't go away. I can't fix it for my kids. I've been trying to fix almost everything, but that's something I just can't."

---

33 Ibid.

34 Stacy Feintuch, "December is Hard."

Lacey Bruno can remember back to the first couple of years after loss. "It was just me and my kid after a family holiday celebration, doing the gifts under the Christmas trees with tears in my eyes." The very first Christmas after her husband died, Lacey and her family rented a house in Orlando. Her son Ricky, and even Lacey, enjoyed the days with the cousins and aunts and uncles. At night, though, everyone coupled up and went their own separate ways with their spouses and families while Lacey and Ricky were alone. "Certainly, no one in my family would want to make me feel less than, but you do."

Fifteen years later, Lacey says that holidays are no longer a great source of pain for her. She and Ricky have created their own rituals and customs, and that is now their new normal.

It is hopeful for me to hear from Lacey that holidays became easier for her with time; because five years later, they are still difficult for me. It is not just the major holidays that stab me in the gut. Even the minor holidays, like Father's Day, Mother's Day, Valentine's day, and birthdays, can be extremely painful.

Debbie Weiss, author of the *Hungover Widow* blog, points out that "the holidays look terrible to us sometimes because they don't look how they're *supposed* to look. But we're the ones who decide what things are *supposed* to look like. Not a Viagra ad, not Plenty of Fish, nor The Hallmark Channel."[35]

---

35 Debbie Weiss, "Coping with Widowhood over the Holidays."

I personally have a picture in my mind of how holidays should look: the Norman Rockwell painting of the mother and father decorating for Christmas as the children prance around the house in blissful ignorance of the cruelness the world can offer. When it is just me and my boys, I feel not only the absence of Chad, but also that my expectations of what life should look like as an adult with young children are not being met. I feel like it is supposed to be different, and I have a hard time moving past the fact that it's just not.

In the section called Surviving the Storm, I offer additional practical ideas about what my sons and I do to make the hard times, like holidays, more manageable. Creating rituals where we take hikes and volunteer on those most difficult days are a couple of things that have helped us. I have also learned a lot from the widows whom I interviewed and read about on my journey writing this book. Some widows go on cruises or exciting vacations over the holidays, so they don't get wrapped up in what no longer is. Some find it helpful to completely avoid social media. Other widows find solace in visiting their loved one's gravesite, or the complete opposite, skipping work and heading to the spa for the day.

On our first Christmas without Chad, only one month after his passing, my girlfriends in the neighborhood purchased the boys' entire Christmas list. The gifts they delivered under our Christmas tree (a gorgeous, full, sweet-smelling tree that our neighbor's son brought home for us from the local nursery as a surprise) were adorned with colorful gold and red paper and elaborate bows and ribbons. It was a huge relief to know that gift purchasing and wrapping was one less thing I needed to focus on amid the endless paperwork, phone calls, grief, and my impending return to work.

That selfless act of kindness that was bestowed upon our family continues to drive me today to help others during the holidays. For the past two years we have been donating toys, gift cards, and money to families who have recently lost a parent. Last year, the family we helped was in our immediate neighborhood. This year, it was a family in need in one of my widow groups. For us, giving to others who are in the same situation that we were in just five years earlier gives us a sense of purpose.

Heather Hofmann's sister helps each Christmas by taking Heather's two boys out shopping for her. The sister finds out what Heather would like, and she takes the boys out for a day of shopping, lunch, and wrapping. What an amazing gift this would be—time alone, presents for you, kids busy!

Friends and family can help in so many big and small ways: wrapping gifts for us, allowing us time to shop or decompress, or inviting us to join them for their holiday dinner so we don't have to be alone. The smallest offer can mean the world to a grieving widow.

December 2021 will be our fifth Christmas without Chad. I would like to do something special to honor him. I found an idea of how to go about this while interviewing Laura Keller. The Kellers celebrate Christmas, and after Joe died, his stocking hung empty. Laura came up with a clever way to fill it. A few weeks before Christmas last year, Laura reached out to Joe's friends and family and asked them to share stories of him.

That Christmas morning, Joe's stocking was filled with letters for the children to read all about their dad and his life before illness. "It was a nice way to bring him into the day," Laura says. I would like to bring Chad into our day like this this coming Christmas. I will be borrowing the Kellers' ritual.

Another wise widow whom I often look toward for inspiration is Michelle Steinke-Baumgard, author of the *One Fit Widow* blog. Michelle's husband, Mitch, died in a plane crash at age thirty-six. Michelle has since remarried, which has posed various challenges during the holidays. In her blog, she shares clever ideas that have helped me to refocus my attention on what is truly important throughout the season.

When Mitch first passed away, Michelle, in her attempt to help her children continue to find joy in the holidays, sometimes overdid them. She says:

> *I made the common mistake of trying to make up for his death by going overboard with stuff under the tree! Nothing I would purchase would ever bring him back, but I naively thought stuff would help, and it gave us all that momentary endorphin rush you get when you are buying new things. I knew deep down inside that monetary gifts could never replace their dad, but that didn't stop me from trying.*[36]

---

36 Michelle Steinke-Baumgard, "Uncluttering our Christmas."

Now that Michelle has remarried, she and her new husband have four children between the two of them. They decided to give up on all the "stuff" and really focus on quality. Michelle now writes a letter to her children and other loved ones each Christmas that paints a picture of what she feels is special about them.[37]

She and her husband gift each of their children only a handful of physical items. Each child receives one personalized ornament and one gift from Santa. Then, all the children partake in a scavenger hunt, scampering around the house, to find out what the big family gift will be. It is always a big family trip somewhere that all will enjoy together. In addition to those three gifts, each child also receives tokens good for alone time with one or both parents or for family time.[38] Steinke-Baumgard modified traditions to fit her new family and life in order to move forward in a way that was joyful for them all.

Holidays are difficult. They can be full of bittersweet reminders of what we no longer have and reminders of what we still do. As time passes, the holidays have gotten easier for me, but there is still always that bit of sadness that mingles with the joy. Changing traditions, mindsets, or venues may be just the shift young widows need in making those most difficult days more manageable and eventually filled with light once again.

---

37 Steinke-Baumgard, "The Christmas Letter."

38 Steinke-Baumgard, "Uncluttering our Christmas."

CHAPTER 6

WIDOW BRAIN

"Retrieving a memory might be a bit like taking ice cream out of the freezer and leaving it in direct sunlight for a while. By the time our memory goes back into the freezer, it might have naturally become a little misshapen."[39]

This sort of memory distortion affects all people to some extent, but forgetfulness and confusion often plague new widows acutely. Many people call this "widow brain" or "widow's fog." It is a phenomenon that most of the young widows whom I spoke with and read about have experienced.

What is widow brain, you may ask? Widow brain is our body's response to trauma, its way of shielding us from our loss. Lisa M. Shulman, MD, author and professor of neurology at the University of Maryland, explains it by saying, "The brain kicks into action to protect us during a traumatic experience. Imagine what would happen if we weren't able to function during traumatic times. To sustain function and

39 Robert Nash, "Are Memories Reliable."

survival, the brain acts as a filter sensing the threshold of emotions and memories that we can and cannot handle."[40]

Widows experience this protective mechanism in multiple ways:

- Numbness
- Forgetfulness
- Lack of physical stamina[41]

In an article written by Kerri Fivecoat-Campbell founder and administrator of a number of widows' Facebook groups, she tells of a fifty-year-old woman, Beth Bridges, whose husband died of heart failure. She remembers how she could not find anything immediately following his death. "I would do things like lose my coffee mug and find it in the refrigerator or my bedroom, unable to remember setting it down there."[42]

I am not immune to widow brain.

The morning after Chad died, I was lying in bed unable to function. My mom came in to see if she could get me anything, and the only thing I could think of was a picture of him. I realized that of all the thousands of pictures floating through my brain, asleep or awake, none of them were of Chad as a healthy person. He had been sick with cancer

40 Lisa Schulman, "Before and After Loss: A Neurologist's Perspective on Loss, Grief and the Brain."

41 Alejandra Vasquez, "What Does it Mean to Have 'Widow Brain' After a Spouse Dies."

42 Kerri Fivecoat-Campbell, "How to Get Through the Fog of Grief."

for five months and his body had grown feeble and weak. All my memories of him captured what used to be his five-foot-eleven, 175-pound frame reduced to what looked like a skeleton with shrunken cheeks, bald head, yellow teeth, and sunken eyes.

As hard as I tried, I could not conjure images of his healthy self, his toothy white smile, his round Irish face and full rosy cheeks, his handsome hazel eyes with lashes so long that some days it looked as if he were wearing mascara. I tried to picture different vacations we had been on, memorable times together, but it was hopeless. I needed a photo of him as a healthy man to jump start my memory.

My mom brought me a picture of Chad and the boys smiling at me from a flowery silver frame. I kept that photo next to my bed for nearly four months before I started having glimpses of him as his old self. Even then, all my memories were freeze framed. Most still are, to be honest. I remember praying to God, "Please let me have a dream about him where he is moving and healthy."

Once, during that time, I did have a dream where Chad was leaning next to an oversized grandfather clock. The pendulum on the clock was broken. Chad was eyeing me intently as I walked toward him, and he smiled. My stomach dropped. It seemed so real, like I was with him again. He was happy to see me. However, as quickly as his smile emerged, it disappeared from his face. He turned his back to me. I screamed out to him, "Look at me! Why are you not looking at me?" He never turned around again.

When I woke up, I was devastated. My heart was racing. I was drenched in sweat, and tears were streaming down my cheeks. He wanted nothing to do with me. He had said nothing.

Then, it dawned on me. He was healthy in my dream and moving! My unconscious mind had at least gifted me that.

Charity Yanishak DeNeal recalls it being around the two-year mark post-loss that she began remembering Drew healthy. Laura Keller, however, five years later says:

> *I have trouble remembering almost anything about him. I have fragments of memories. I can't remember the feeling of having a healthy unbroken family. I was married for over twenty years. It's like I'm living a totally different life. I was a person with young children and a husband, and now I'm a single person with older children. It's like a guillotine came down and cut off that part of my life.*

I typically picture Chad healthy now. When I see pictures of him sick, I'm taken aback. I do, however, agree with Laura that it is like I am a different person living a different life. Once upon a time, there was a young woman named Audra who was married to a wonderful man named Chad, and they had young twin boys.

She disappeared.

Now, there exists a forty-something single woman named Audra who has two adolescent boys. As time passes, each woman becomes more and more distinct from the other.

Last July would have been our nineteenth wedding anniversary, and my son and I were looking though the wedding album. It was peppered with pictures of typical wedding highlights: the walk down the aisle, the first dance, the toast, cutting the cake. The main characters in this book were both young and sweet, with a pinch of naivete that enhanced the dreamlike mood of joy that was palpable as we flipped through the pages. But the twenty-four-year-old girl in those pictures was not me. Not the me I know now. They could have been photos of someone else in as much as I could connect emotionally to them. I am detached from that old self, those old memories.

Grief has not only impacted my ability to access my memories, but also my ability to organize thoughts. Most of my young widow tribe will speak freely about the difficulty they have focusing on day-to-day tasks and keeping order in their lives. There is so much to do when a spouse dies, from wills to probate, bills to pay, credit card and bank accounts to cancel, death certificates to order and distribute, jobs to keep, children's schedules to maintain, and grief to manage.

At the beginning, grief prevented my mind from focusing on anything for more than a few minutes. I found lists extremely helpful, electronic calendars, telling people to "remind me" when I knew I would forget before I could get to a piece of paper or the notes section of my iPhone.

This haze eventually faded, but it took a couple of years. I still often feel like my concentration is not as strong as it used to be, and I have to put forth a great deal of effort to stay present. I forget words for concepts that used to flow off my tongue easily. Just the other day, I accidentally switched my boys' medicine so that one of them took too high a dose, and I had to call poison control. I am less sharp.

Jacob Brown, a marriage and family therapist in California, says it can take two to three months to emerge from the fog, but often it takes even longer.[43]

It is surprising how often I still forget that I am a widow, that my kids have lost their father, or that I have lost my best friend and husband. Maybe "forget" is not the right word, but it is often not in my immediate consciousness. When I met my friend Heather, she told me her story of losing her husband, Ralf. My heart hurt so much for her and her boys, and I cried thinking of them navigating this world alone. The first words out of my mouth as I sat across from her in the noisy Chop't restaurant with people happily buzzing around us were, "I can't even imagine."

Wait. Yes, I can. I am living it.

The same reaction came when my friends Andrea, Melanie, Lacey, and all the women in my grief group told their stories. As much as we think about our lost loved ones multiple times a day, the full reality of their eternal absence may not truly hit us until we are in the midst of someone else living the same reality. Or, unexpectedly on a rainy Sunday at 2:35 p.m. I never really know when my widow brain will sharpen and stab me in the gut.

---

43 Ibid.

C.S. Lewis, Christian anthropologist and renowned author of the famous series *Chronicles of Narnia*, wrote an amazingly introspective book after his wife died called *A Grief Observed*. "How often" he wonders, "will the vast emptiness astonish me like a complete novelty and make me say, I never realized my loss 'til this moment. The same leg is cut off time after time. The first plunge of the knife into the flesh is felt again and again."[44]

The saddest part to me is that my memory keeper is gone. Someone will say, "Remember when..." and often my answer is, "No, not exactly." The one who could have set it straight, my husband, is no longer here. Chad and I knew each other for twenty-plus years. If my memory was vague, I would ask him to bring it back into focus. It was comforting and peaceful knowing that someone else shared those experiences and could reconstruct what needed to be made whole. Now, things that happened in the past will forever be lost there because I forget them. I am the last in line as the keeper of a long string of memories we had created together.

Our brains and bodies are incredible machines. They protect us from emotions that are too painful to feel all at once. But over time, they let us in on the reality of our situation.

Dr. Alejandra Vasquez, a certified grief counselor, acknowledges that, "When you allow the process of grief to take its course without trying to suppress it, you'll find that things get easier to manage as time goes on. Your grief and sorrow

---

44 C.S. Lewis, *A Grief Observed,* Read by Douglas Gresham, Audible, 2014, Audible audio ed., 1:30:55.

will gradually lift, and you'll start to feel better." This is one of the reasons that therapists advise us to take a year before making any rash decisions.[45]

Michelle Steinke-Baumgard, in her book *Healthy Healing*, maintains that exercise and sleep are critical in clearing the fog. She explains how, when we sleep, our "blood pressure plummets, the extra mental 'trash' you accumulate during the day gets cleared out, and of course your body creates important growth hormones." When it is difficult to sleep, as it often is when grief is raw, she recommends exercise. Exercise has the ability to promote sleep by physically exhausting us as well as decreasing our stress and anxiety.[46]

Understanding that widow brain is not unique to me has helped me embrace and accept it. In retrospect, I am thankful that it protected me in the beginning from experiencing the tidal wave of simultaneous emotions. It made me slow down when I would have plowed full speed ahead without processing my grief. When it still afflicts me, and it does, I become frustrated. We are coming to terms with each other though, developing an understanding that we both have the same goal of helping me survive, enjoy my life, and raise my children.

---

45 Vasquez, "What Does it Mean to Have 'Widow Brain.'"

46 Michelle Steinke-Baumgard, *Healthy Living: A Guide to Working Out Grief*, 42.

CHAPTER 7

FEAR, ANXIETY, AND YOUR HEALTH

"When we lose our tolerance for vulnerability, joy becomes foreboding."

~ BRENÉ BROWN

Brené Brown, a research professor at the University of Houston who studies courage, vulnerability, shame, and empathy, explains how we as humans say, "I'm not going to soften into this moment of joy because I'm scared it's going to be taken away." She maintains that "we are trying to dress rehearse tragedy so that we can beat vulnerability to the punch." This dress rehearsal happens in so many ways for widows.[47]

At first, when Chad died, my fears circled around basic needs. For instance, what would happen if I needed to lift something

---

47 Brené Brown, "Dr. Brené Brown on Joy: It's Terrifying."

I couldn't? How would I do the lawn chores? How does one pay the bills? Life 101.

As time went on, I worked out how to solve these problems (thanks, YouTube and Dad). The more problems I solved, the less fear I had around conquering life's basic duties.

Andrea Albanese talks about her anxiety teaching her oldest how to drive:

> *Okay, I'm gonna put up a good fight and show my son that Mom's got it, even though inside I'm going, 'Oh, I really don't have this.' At the time it's incredibly overwhelming. And then when I get through it, it's like another step of competence. I don't like it, but I've come to accept it, and I know that I can do it.*

New challenges still scare me. When it comes time to teach my boys to drive, I will be terrified. And five years out, it still often feels like I am waiting for the other shoe to drop. Although I no longer have as much anxiety around basic life duties, I continue to find myself envisioning the worst about our future. I worry if we will be able to live off the life insurance money that was left for us, or if I will be able to afford college for my kids. My greatest worry is that something will happen to me that will take me away from my children.

Last Christmas, my eye was twitching, and I felt pressure behind it. I spent days clicking on every related link on the internet before concluding that I had a brain tumor and that 2020 would in fact be my last year of life. I made an appointment with my primary doctor because my usual eye doctor was closed for the holidays. I pulled into the driveway of the doctor's office that sat adjacent to the parking lot of the hospital where I had come every day for a week to visit my husband who was awaiting a cancer diagnosis.

A huge wave of sadness and dread swept over me. I found the closest parking spot, pulled in, and let loose that ugly cry that contorts my face and makes me look like something inhuman. I didn't want to cry too hard or for too long because that would make my eyes puffy and red to the point where the doctor who was going to examine me would send me home with a vial of Zoloft instead of an antibiotic eye drop.

I tried hard to dam up the river, to think of happy thoughts or talk myself out of anything I had previously talked myself into. But I couldn't. It took me about ten minutes to calm myself down with deep breathing and loud unattractive nose blowing.

Once my primary doctor looked me over, she surmised that nothing was wrong. To rule everything out, she ended up sending me to the ophthalmologist across the hall. It turned out that my eye was fine, and the stress and anxiety of the holidays had likely brought it on. The eye doctor also assured me that I had no cause to believe that I had a brain tumor. *Phew.*

This particular experience happened over four years after my husband passed away. Incidents like it happened many times before that, and I imagine they will happen many times after. The therapist I was seeing when it first occurred diagnosed it as "white coat syndrome" or "white coat hypertension."

White coat syndrome is a physical symptom where a person's blood pressure spikes due to fear and anxiety related to doctor visits. I'm not sure if that physically happens to me, but I can tell you that I have cried many times outside and inside of doctor's offices since Chad died.[48]

I cried when I had an abnormal mammogram and after returning for the second time the doctor told me I was all clear. I cried when my primary doctor told me that maybe things were too much for me, and I should consider an anti-depressant. I cried when my cardiologist told me that the heart pains I was experiencing were likely stress after doing every test on me that he could imagine. I cried when my pap smear came back abnormal, and I had to go back to get a biopsy of my cervix. I cried when I almost passed out at the gym and the ambulance had to take me to the hospital.

Part of this was likely white coat syndrome from the experiences I had for five months in and out of hospitals with Chad, but a huge part was relief. Like many of my friends who are widows, I live in a constant state of fear that I will also die early. I am terrified of the idea that my children could, in an instant, become orphans, and that the only people who will be there to take care of them will be my aging parents and in-laws who will eventually leave them as well. I've read the research about how repeated loss and trauma makes recovery more futile for children. This cannot be the fate of my boys.

My fear is not based purely on emotion. A proven phenomenon called the "widowhood effect" is very real. According to

---

48 Richard Sine, "Beyond 'White Coat Syndrome.'"

a study led by Paul Boyle out of the University of St. Andrews in Scotland, for up to ten years after the death of a spouse, the widow or widower is at a 40 percent higher risk of death than the non-widow. A study out of Johns Hopkins, led by Cardiologist Ilan Wittstein, discovered that a phenomenon in widows and widowers called "broken heart syndrome" can actually make your heart muscles weaker. Widows and widowers are five times more likely than their peers to experience heart failure. Middle-aged and elderly widows are most likely to develop this condition.[49]

I had heart palpitations intermittently throughout my life, but when Chad died, my heart went haywire. The beats were abnormal, and a new symptom emerged. My heart physically hurt. I went to the cardiologist multiple times, wore Holter monitors, took stress tests, EKGs, and ultrasounds; the doctors could find nothing wrong with me aside from my usual, harmless arrhythmia. I asked the doctors if the pain could be related to my loss and grief. They said that it could be stress-related. I can't think of many situations more stress-inducing.

I started asking my widow friends about their health in relation to their losses. Andrea Albanese notes, "What I didn't expect after him dying was all of the physical pain. I felt my grief at a physical level." The subject of heart issues and physical pain often emerged from these conversations, normally in the context of a newfound anxiety.

---

49 "Widowhood Can Shorten a Partner's Lifespan."

Laura Keller says she is paranoid because the stakes seem so much higher now if she were to get sick. "If something happens to me, we are screwed. There are people around, but ultimately they are my kids, and I have to take care of them."

She tells the story of how she had a physical when Joe got sick, covering her bases to make sure that she, as the only healthy parent, was actually healthy. Her results came back normal, and she was told that she was in good health.

Then, Joe died.

Laura started having heart palpitations that she attributed to menopause. But, as time went on, they started to get worse, and she began to worry. She went back to the doctor, now four months after her original visit. She had an abnormal EKG this time, and her blood pressure was shockingly high.

"How can this be?" the doctor asked. "I just saw you four months ago. Has anything happened in your life between now and then?" Laura went, as she describes it, to "crazy town." She burst into tears as she struggled to explain her situation. When the doctor heard her story, he diagnosed her with "situational high blood pressure." Her loss had literally sent her blood pressure skyrocketing.

Dr. Carlo Carandang, a psychiatrist specializing in anxiety and depression and founder of AnxietyBoss.com[2] notes that a study by Tudiver and others found that widows under the age of sixty-five actually tend to have worse anxiety than older widows. But, after around seven months, much of the fear and anxiety lessens.[50] I'm not a psychiatrist, but I think this happens for a number of reasons.

Widows are masters at figuring out how to regain control of their lives in any ways they are able. We can't bring our spouses back, but we sure as hell can repaint rooms, redo kitchens, or move homes. So many of my widow friends found healing in clearing out or renovating their houses.

Laura Keller renovated all the major areas in her home. She says, "Now it doesn't feel so bad because I can't picture him in that room. It looks entirely different now than when he lived there."

I did many home improvement projects when Chad passed as well. One reason is we had moved into an older house only two years prior, and we couldn't afford to fix it up then. Also, I needed a fresh start like Laura did. I could not, nor would Chad want me to, live in a home that was a shrine frozen in time. I continue to display his picture in many of our rooms, and I always will. However, the house looks quite different now than it did five years ago.

Elisabeth Kübler-Ross says, "Control gives us the illusion of safety and helps us think we are holding everything together." But she likens it to salt, "a dab of it can make something a little better, but too much can spoil it completely."[51]

---

50 Carlo Carandang, "How Being Widowed Affects Your Anxiety."

51 Elisabeth Kübler-Ross and David Kessler, *On Grief*, 95-97.

I think the furthest I went with this need for control was getting Lasix done on my eyes. I used to be blind as a bat. I could not see my alarm next to my bed. I would roll over when it would sound, feel around for my glasses, and put them on so that I could gain my bearings.

When Chad died, the lack of control that my poor eyesight caused scared me to death. What if an intruder came in the house, and I couldn't get to my glasses soon enough? Or worse, what if one of my children were drowning, and I couldn't save him because I couldn't see him?

So, I went to see Lasix surgeon Dr. Roy Rubinfeld. Dr. Rubinfeld was a kind, extroverted man, filled with life stories. During my consult visit, I told him about my fears, and he told me a story about a soldier whose eyesight he corrected.

This soldier would have reoccurring nightmares that he was down in a hole with a gun. Each night in his dream, someone came to the top of the hole. The soldier couldn't see if this person were friendly or the enemy. He was terrified to shoot and terrified not to shoot. His poor eyesight gave him anxiety even in his dreams.

I could relate not only to the soldier's need to be able to protect himself and others, but also the lack of control he felt in not being capable to do so. This man understood me. There was no looking back for me after that. I had my eyesight corrected days later.

When COVID-19 emerged, my fears quadrupled. I watched videos of women whose young and old husbands went into the emergency room with various symptoms and never returned. These stories sent me into a panic. I see-sawed between believing that I had some sort of comorbidity that would make the virus kill me or being convinced that the stomach bug I had back in February was actually COVID and now I had the antibodies.

If I got sick, no one would be able to help me. My parents couldn't come. They were in their seventies. Our friends would not want to be exposed. We would have to go this alone. I started making extra portions of every dinner so I could freeze food for my boys to eat if I got sick.

One morning I woke up at 4:00 a.m. from a fitful sleep where I had clenched my teeth so hard that I put a hole in the night guard that I wear. I immediately started crying. I felt completely helpless and knew that I could not function well in this state.

I remembered Michelle Steinke-Baumgard's post on her *One Fit Widow* blog about how the one thing she wished her husband had done for their children before he had died was something she herself still had not done seven years later—write them a letter.[52] I had taken her lead after I read this a couple of years prior to the pandemic because one of my regrets also was that Chad had not written to the boys or made them a video. I had two letters already for each boy in my file cabinet, sealed and labeled with their names on them. They were handwritten so that they have my personal

52 Michelle Steinke-Baumgard, "The Christmas Letter."

flair. I had the time to hand-write those first letters. I didn't feel this looming fear of dying.

That morning, though, I needed to get the words out quickly. I needed to write down everything swimming around in my head before I lost it. I grabbed my computer and typed for two hours.

I printed the letters and sealed the envelopes, and I felt like a weight had lifted. I put them in the file drawer with the others and texted two close friends and my mom to let them know they were there. I closed the drawer on my feeling of helplessness. This small act allowed me a glimmer of control once again.

I believe the anxiety can eventually subside for widows once we form a relationship with our bodies as well. Both Heather Hofmann and Charity Yanishak DeNeal describe physical symptoms brought on by grief-related anxiety. Heather says, "I start to get pain in my jaw and then it turns into shooting pains in my shoulder and my back. I think I am having a heart attack, and I think, *My kids won't know how much I loved them*!"

Charity describes a similar sensation, "I have pressure and pain sitting on my chest. I don't want to do anything. My neck will act up and it starts to radiate down my arm."

Both women clearly articulate the patterns that their bodies follow when anxiety arises. They now understand the root cause. At first, they were terrified they too were dying. Soon, they realized that their bodies were leaving them clues to remind them to take a break and be mindful.

For three years, every June, I thought I had a terminal disease. My breathing would become shallow, and I felt shortness of breath even as I sat. My heart palpitations would resume, and I felt exhausted, like I had the flu. As much as I always tell myself that lightning does not strike twice in the same place, I was terrified. Having not yet determined that this was a pattern of anxiety, I would go to the doctor every June. One year, my doctor told me that I was likely depressed, and she put me on anti-depression medications. All the prescription did was make me so tired that I could not parent or stay awake. So, I stopped taking them.

This year, I had an epiphany. June is a crappy month. It is the end of school, which brings about painful benchmarks. June is Chad's birthday. It is Father's Day. It is the month that Chad was diagnosed with cancer. Why did it take me so long to realize this?

This year, I leaned into my June grief and anxiety. I did not stress over any of the big days. We made Chad's favorite meal for his birthday, took a hike for Father's Day, and generally took it much easier than we had in the past. I had always felt like I had to go overboard in memory of him. This year, though, I realized that he would just want us to be happy.

I see a lot of posts on the young widows Facebook groups where a young widow says she is going to live like her husband would have wanted her to. I understand the idea behind this, and I do it myself. She wants to honor him properly.

However, he is no longer here. We, their widows, are the ones who are still here. I now realize I need to do what is best for us, myself and my children. We have been through a lot. We must take care of ourselves so that we can live long, productive lives. Our health and well-being must be first and foremost. I have begun replacing the "shoulds" with the "coulds." Life is much healthier and more enjoyable when I allow myself some flexibility and open up to possibility.

CHAPTER 8

UNCOUPLING

One of the hardest parts of losing a spouse is losing half of yourself. Not only did I lose Chad, but I lost Audra and Chad. The us, the we, the Mr. and Mrs. Whether you didn't get along with your spouse or he was your best friend, in marriage the couple is often seen as a singular. When your partner dies, are you now only half? A fraction of who you used to be?

Women become single in many ways. Some are married and no longer love their spouses. Some are divorced. Some are widowed. Whatever leads a person to this place of singleness, she mourns her future, the life she envisioned as she stood across from her partner and repeated her wedding vows. Those dreams are out of reach now, and yet she continues to long for that happily ever after.

As the surviving spouse, there are other dimensions of emptiness as well. Your best friend is gone, your confidant, your secret keeper, your lover, your hand holder, your idea bouncer, maybe your income provider, your mechanic, your handyman. Who is going to be all of that for you now?

For many, the answer is simple: You are.

In Sheryl Sandburg and Adam Grant's book, *Option B*, Sandburg quotes an old adage, "Let me fall if I must fall. The one I become will catch me."[53]

This has been true for me. When Chad first died, I was terrified of doing many things alone, especially the bills. In our fourteen-plus years of marriage, certain parts of the division of labor were very clear. Chad dealt with the garbage, the yard, the bills, and anything that needed to be fixed. I, in turn, was in charge of everything else (I'm joking, of course, but only kind of).

One thing for certain was that I did not have *any* idea how to use the online banking program with which Chad so diligently tracked our finances. When doctors diagnosed Chad with cancer and things did not seem to be improving, I bombarded him with questions about passcodes, electronic bill pay, and automatic withdraws. The poor man did not even roll his eyes or sigh as he showed me for the thousandth and first time how it all worked. I just could not get the hang of it. I think my amygdala (that primitive part of our brains that senses fear) took over, and it paralyzed me from learning anything.

When he finally passed, I was convinced I could not do this. I asked his dad, his brother, and my dad all for help, but no one really knew his intricate system, and people are funny about meddling in other people's finances.

---

53 Sheryl Sandberg and Adam Grant, *Option B*, 80.

So, I figured it out.

After a few months of not knowing which bills were being paid, deadlines being missed, and late fees accrued, I finally determined how to cancel electronic bills and pay outstanding bills, and I shut down his system.

Done.

I moved to a basic system that my bank offered, and I have never looked back.

This need to learn in order to fill Chad's mighty large shoes has been a repetitive theme for the past five years. From learning how to work an elaborate speaker system, putting chains on bikes, unclogging drains, and plunging toilets, I have had to step into the traditional male roles. It has been rewarding, but it can be utterly exhausting being two people at once.

When my friend Charity Yanishak DeNeal lost her husband, Drew, she said she felt lost and overwhelmed. "For six months before and six months after, you are just in a gray haze. You are just trying to get through each day."

Heather Hofmann says, "During the day, I feel fine. It's nighttime that's the hardest. I feel isolated and singled out, and I get anticipational anxiety about going out anywhere, even with my best friends. They never make me feel bad, but I feel like I'm the odd man out." However, Heather, like many widows, tries to say yes to invitations as much as possible;

because she fears that if she says no too much, she may stop being invited. "I get scared that I will be 'that widow.'"

Lacey Bruno, who lost her husband fifteen years ago, says, "For years, you don't get included, you don't get invited places. I'd get invited to girls' nights kind of stuff, but not the couples' parties."

Sometimes the most difficult part is not even the fear of missing out, but the pain that it causes to be there at all. Melanie Green says it bluntly, "I hate it. It's just very lonely. I do feel jealous when I see other couples." Normally, Melanie's kids offer her a buffer, and she can use them to keep busy at social events. However, she has forced herself to go to two or three gatherings where only adults were in attendance. She feels vulnerable. "It's very hard to walk into a room without Jon. I feel extremely self-conscious, like all eyes are on me. Jon was my other half, my shield, my armor."

Laura Keller mirrors those feelings. "Everyone in the neighborhood is a couple. They invite me, but it's hard to go and watch all of the couples."

Kelley Rogers, a widow friend in my community, can remember her father sharing these feelings at her mother's funeral years ago. "I remember my dad saying, 'We turned away from the gravesite, and you kids, every one of you, grabbed the hand of your partner, your spouse, and began to walk. I reached for your mom's hand, and I realized then that I would never ever have a hand to grab again.'" Kelley's husband Jon went missing a few years ago. When the authorities found him weeks later, they presumed he had died from a fall while attempting to extricate his car from a steep pitch. Kelley is now able to relate firsthand to that feeling of loneliness and separateness that her father described those years before.

Even school events can elicit these types of emotions, not necessarily because people are coupled, but because all around us we see families that, in the traditional sense, are considered "whole." It's funny, because when I break apart the crowd in my mind later, I realize that the auditorium was filled with families with two dads, a single mother whose child has never met his father, a father who is battling brain cancer, a mother and a father who refuse to sit near each other because they are in the midst of a nasty divorce, and other dynamics exist that I know nothing about. But when I simply scan the room, it feels like it is filled with rainbows and unicorns, and I enter dragging the storm cloud with me. Other people likely don't even notice. But I do.

Kelley also brings up a key point that not only is it difficult for us to forge this new normal without a partner, but it's also difficult for others too. People often do not know what to say. At first, most people are comfortable telling you they are sorry for your loss. But as time goes on, if they had never had the chance to tell you early on, it seems to become more awkward for them. Eventually, it becomes the gigantic elephant in the room. Clearly, you both know that your husband died. Not a day goes by when I forget that my husband is no longer with me and my children, and typically the person I am talking to has not forgotten either. Sometimes, I just bring it up to clear the air and make it more comfortable for the other person. Not for me, but for them.

The loss of your other half can bankrupt you of your physical partner and of everything you knew life to be. Hurt stems not only from the loss of this actual person, but also from your new family status. People are often invited to events based upon their relationships. Some women decide if they want to put effort into a friendship with another woman based upon whether the men would get along or not. Families are invited or not invited to barbecues and vacations with some families based upon the similarity of the family structure.

It is both scary and sad to think that some of my favorite times will never feel complete again. I am on my own trying to navigate vacations. Unless we go with another family, there is no other adult to sit and have a glass of wine with or unwind with at the end of the day. I often wish that we would be invited on more vacations with other families, but usually the husband wants to have a comrade too, and I don't have that to offer. Also, sometimes I just like to be with my immediate family, not with others all the time. This is the vacation paradox that I run into every time I think about planning a trip.

The most heartbreaking piece of uncoupling is the toll it takes on my children.

Kids notice the subtle changes in their family. A child who has been touched by the loss of a parent is not immune to the ripples that the wounded family structure creates. Often through social constructs themselves, they are excluded or inadvertently made to feel less: Donuts for Dads, Father-Daughter dances, or Father's Day card decorating in the classroom, just to name a few. Even just words and phrases used thoughtlessly, "Ask your mom and dad," or, "Tell your dad to help you with (fill in the blank of whatever stereotypically male activity needs to be completed)." For children who don't have a mom or dad anymore, these simple phrases are a slap in the face.

Andrea Phipps, a fellow widow whom I met through a mutual friend, lost her husband Michael when he was struck by an automobile. She was thirty years old. After Michael's death, Andrea no longer thought of herself and her two girls as a family anymore. She had always been part of what she considered a traditional family herself.

For ten years, on the return address labels of her Christmas cards, Andrea wrote, "The Phipps Girls" followed by their address. Then one year she said, "I am not giving myself credit. We ***are*** actually a family. I don't know why it was, and I don't know when, but I realized just because we are not a traditional family, it doesn't mean we're not a family at all." After that, her return address labels identified the ladies as what they actually are, "The Phipps Family."

Heather Hofmann was in a therapy session, and she told her therapist how much she missed wearing her wedding rings. "They made me feel like a part of something, like I belonged to something."

The therapist asked Heather if she had anything to represent the new tribe she belonged to without Ralf. She was stunned. "What new tribe?"

The therapist explained that she and her boys are now the tribe. She offered the idea of finding something to signify *their* bond, something she could wear close like she did her wedding band.

This shift in thinking was what Heather needed to focus less on what was missing and more on what was being created.

Heather continues to contemplate what this new tribal symbol should be. She knows she wants it to be a piece of jewelry that she can wear daily with some sort of sign of her love for her boys. She hasn't landed yet on exactly what that will look like.

For adults and children alike, the uncoupling of the pair and the change in family structure affects us in so many ways. Vacations are different, holidays are different, weekends are different, even simple school and neighborhood events are different. I have recently begun to see different in a more positive light. My new tribe may not be the tribe I had imagined as a child, but we *are* perfectly whole.

SECTION III.

THE CREW

"The little reed, bending to the force of the wind, soon stood upright again when the storm had passed over."

—AESOP

CHAPTER 9

RESILIENCE

Many times, in the decade before Chad died, I could remember driving by the Robert A. Pumphrey funeral home thinking it was the most beautiful building on the block. A vast green lawn divides the stately white building from the bustling main street. The bushes and white and pink flowers skirting the front of the home are always impeccably manicured.

As a child, my mom said that funeral homes are consistently the best-looking buildings on the block, and from my experience, she is correct. However, driving up to this same building on November 30, 2015, beauty was not what I saw. I saw the place where my husband's dead body was being held before it was converted to ash. I felt nervous, nauseous, and unstable.

"Hello, Mrs. O'Neil," the funeral director said as he met us at the door. I introduced him to my mother, who had accompanied me.

He led us into the foyer that was connected to a family room. It looked like a room from a 1970s sitcom with its yellowed floral couches, dark wood tables, and chairs with ornate legs that jutted out invitingly. The stale smell that permeates old homes struck me first: the smell of death and decay.

Adjacent to the foyer was a grand staircase that we ascended on our way to the funeral director's unassuming office. Two chairs sat across from a small wooden desk where the director perched himself and took out a green leather-bound binder.

"I'm sorry for your loss, Mrs. O'Neil." He paused for a moment and then continued. "Could you tell me a little about Chad?"

Being foreign to death myself, with my grandmother, a couple of dogs, and our friend Drew being the extent of my experience, I couldn't help but think how graceful the funeral director was in the way he spoke about Chad. After answering a number of his questions and filling out paperwork, the director caught me off guard.

"Someone has to see the body before we cremate him."

What? I don't know why I didn't realize this was a thing. I saw him die with my own eyes. I held his hand as all the parts of his body that had once served him so well, failed.

I knew he had died. Why did I have to view the shell that was left behind? The way I saw it, he was no longer in there.

"And," he continued, "this is when people often have close friends and family come to pay their last respects, for closure, before the service."

Oh.

This added a whole different logistical angle. His family and mine were already at my house. Should I invite our closest friends? How do I define closest? And then came the real RKO (as my kids would say before they knock someone out in a video game), "Do you want your children to see him?"

My initial response was, "*Lord, no*!" I was thirty-nine years old and had only ever been to two funerals. The last thing I thought my kids needed was to see their father's body lying in a casket.

The director handed me a tri-fold pamphlet and said, "Think about it. Sometimes it is good to give children choices in these situations."

That night, I read that pamphlet back and front multiple times. It offered helpful insight into supporting children throughout each and every step of this difficult experience. I googled "should kids see a dead parent?" Most of the research agreed that being allowed to be a part of all pieces of the after-death arrangements helped them say goodbye and understand the finality.

That pamphlet made me realize I needed to tell my children as much of the truth as they were ready for. Otherwise, they might invent other realities themselves, realities that may be worse than the truth. All I wanted to do at that time was protect them from more pain, but I learned that choosing whether or not they would see their father after death allowed them to feel part of everything and that they would have some say or control in it all.[54]

So, I approached my twin seven-year-old boys, Matthew and Connor, separately and asked them what they wanted to do. I explained that Daddy had gone to Heaven, and that his soul was all around us. His body was all that was left behind. Did they want to see his body before it was cremated? To my surprise, both confidently said, "Yes."

We decided together what sorts of things they may want to send him off with. Connor found a yellow heart with orange trim (his favorite colors) that he had made from Perler beads. Matthew drew a picture of Chad. Both chose to include a photograph of our family when we were all healthy and whole.

On the night of the viewing, all our closest friends and family gathered in the living room of the funeral home. The funeral director asked me to come alone into the room off the foyer. I walked in and across the room was a basic wooden casket, the kind you see in the movies where prisoners are all being buried en masse.

I held my breath as I approached. What would meet my eyes? I was almost thankful when I looked in. The body that lay

54 Funeral Service Foundation, *Youth and Funerals: Understanding the Important Role Funerals and Memorialization Play in the Lives of Youth* (Wisconsin: Funeral Service Foundation, 2020), 2.

inside looked nothing like my Chad. I could breathe. I could survive watching my kids see him. His head was Mr. Clean bald, unlike it was when he was alive, even after we had to shave his hair when it started to fall out following chemotherapy. Cancer had done such a job on him that his skeletal face and body resembled that of someone else.

Before asking the boys to enter, I set out a cup full of colored sharpies. When I went out to get them, I told them exactly what I had seen and that it was okay if they wanted to change their minds. Neither did.

We entered together. They paused at the casket, both just staring at the body in front of them for a couple of beats.

"You can touch him," I said. "He's not there anymore."

As seven-year-old boys do, they poked and prodded the cold stiff arms and face, they lifted and dropped his hands. Eventually I figured it bordered on harassment to the dead, and I reminded them to be gentle.

They placed their pictures and artwork on his chest, and Connor somehow pinned his picture to the coffin where Chad could see it when it closed. With different colored Sharpies, Matthew and Connor penned their final goodbyes to the father whose body they would never see or feel again: the arms that once encircled them in bear hugs and tossed them high into the air, the back that they climbed on for piggy back rides, the face that they had studied as infants as a guide for how to act, react, and communicate.

Matthew wrote "Bye-Bye, Daddy" in his best handwriting. Connor, "I love you, Daddy," and he framed his with a big orange heart. Those final messages from my sons to their father will forever be frozen in my memory.

According to the Hospice Foundation, children begin to understand that death is final around the ages of eight or nine years old. Before that, children often believe that the deceased are going to return and all will be well again.[55] My boys were seven years old, but they understood the finality, possibly because Connor's godfather, Drew, had passed away two years earlier and they had watched Drew's young girls cope.

Even though they were so young, I'm glad that I gave the boys the opportunity to choose that day. For a long time, I questioned my decision. Should seven-year-olds have been given such a developmentally mature choice?

They are now twelve, and I have asked them since if they wished they hadn't seen their dad looking like that. They both agree that they are glad they had the experience.

We will all experience loss and grief in life, unfortunately some earlier than others. According to the *Journal of Hospice & Palliative Nursing*, in 2008, one and a half million US children had experienced the death of a parent. They predict

55 "Children & Grief," Hospice Foundation of America.

that one out of every twenty children will lose one or both parents before the age of sixteen.[56]

Neale Daniher, a motivational speaker with a degenerative disease, says, "In life, it's not if it gets tough—it's just when and how often."[57]

For my children, and I would imagine for the many others, the loss of their parent was the first major trial in their lives. It will not be their last. From that day to this, my boys continue to shock and amaze me with their resilience and ability to bounce back from the hard things that life throws at them. Life will not always be easy, and the absence of their dad will always be there. However, I hope beyond measure that they will carry the resilience they built as seven-year-old boys with them throughout their long and healthy lives.

---

56 Darrell Owens, "Recognizing the Needs of Bereaved Children in Palliative Care," 14-16.

57 Neale Daniher, "Fight MND," Melbourne Football Club, streamed live on June 5, 2019, YouTube video: 1:25.

CHAPTER 10

HELPING THEM HEAL

The same week as the viewing, I walked into the church where we were to hold Chad's service in order to plan the details—such a strange thing for a thirty-nine-year-old woman to be doing in a church. I was in that post-death haze and didn't particularly want to be alone with myself and my thoughts, so I began searching the barren waiting room for something to occupy my mind.

There was a small table between two wooden benches and scattered upon it were piles of Christian educational materials. I am not a highly religious individual, so none of them interested me, aside from a thin set of papers stapled together peeking out from behind the commercial pamphlets. In the title were the words "Grieving Children." Of course, this was the most important topic on my mind, so I picked it up and began reading. What I read sent chills down my spine and instilled in me a fear worse than death.

It said that children will not only grieve the parent who died, but they will grieve the parent who lives on and is no longer the way she or he used to be.

Oh. *No way.* I could not allow my children to feel this way.

So many of my choices today are based upon my fierce, hostile refusal to allow my children to experience what was written in that one line of text. I plan trips for them, schedule play dates, play games, and adopt puppies. I stretch myself well out of my comfort zone so they are able to stay in theirs, so they will never have to grieve the loss of who I once was to them.

My number one priority after my husband passed away, and after all the most pressing issues were taken care of, was my children. They continue to be my top priority today. Helping them grow around their grief and heal from the loss of their father has taken many shapes.

When Drew died, my friend Charity purchased Daddy Boxes for her girls. I borrowed her idea when Chad died. I went to the Container Store and bought large, solid, clear boxes with lids to keep out dust and moisture. They had wheels on the feet so a seven-year-old boy could easily roll it from beneath his bed to investigate its contents.

Throughout the year after Chad died, I cleaned out various areas of the house little by little. Seven months after his passing, on his birthday in June, I decided to take on his closet. This was the closet that I had crumbled in, curled up into a ball on the floor while hugging my knees and smelling his sweatshirts. This closet was where his maroon survivor's shirt from the Multiple Myeloma Research Foundation race that we had attended only two weeks before he died still hung on a hanger. Still grasping firmly to it were a sticker and a ribbon that he was given for participating. This closet was *hard* to clean out.

One of the things that got me through the process was the sharing. I put all his T-shirts and hats in a line on my bed and took pictures of them. I chose to keep the few that he always wore and reminded me of him. Next, I allowed the boys to choose whichever their favorites were and take them for their Daddy Boxes. After that, I sent the pictures to his three older brothers and his friend Anthony. They each chose what they wanted, and the rest went into a black trash bag to go to the Salvation Army.

His suits, belts, work shoes, and ties (except for a couple of my favorites) went to an organization called A Wider Circle. The boys and I took the professional attire there where they would donate it to men who needed a job and train them with interviewing skills. What a great way to honor Chad.

There were boxes in his closet as well. One was filled with belongings that his friend Oliver had cleared out of his office at Marriott. I had glanced in it when Oliver first delivered it to us, but I had never fully unpacked it. The boys and I took a separate day to really take time remembering what he had in there. Because we didn't visit his office often, and it was always a special adventure when the boys were allowed to go, they held those items in the highest esteem.

There were many memories evoked: The red puzzle ball that was comprised of hundreds of little pieces ("Remember when Dad told us that story about how Oliver threw this ball in his office and it all shattered to pieces?"); or the mug that we gave him on Father's Day with pictures of Chad and the boys on it ("I remember when we gave him this mug!"); the picture of the boys apple picking in a mahogany wood frame ("Oh, wow! I forgot he kept that picture of us in his office.") They chose the favorite items linked to their own personal memories, and those went into their boxes.

This went on as I progressed through the year and through the rooms of the house. His home office held many pictures and awards that the boys were excited to get their hands on. The basement was a treasure trove of memories from when Chad was a boy. Boy Scout Pinewood Derby cars and badges, piano and soccer trophies...the list was endless. The Daddy Boxes filled.

Still, five years later, not a month goes by that Matthew does not take out his Daddy Box to fidget with something in it. He often redecorates his room with the items in the box, putting away things that have been on display and setting out things that have not. Each year when we do the MMRF race in Chad's honor, Matthew and Connor both add trophies and medals to their boxes. Sometimes they discover hidden treasures in drawers and cabinets around the house that none of us have seen in years, and they add them as well.

Chad loved expensive pens, but we could not afford luxuries like these when he was living. He had been given one for graduation from college and one from his team at Marriott. He cherished these pens. These I keep in a special place for when the boys themselves graduate from college. I know that these graduation gifts will mean more to them than any other material item ever could.

In addition to sharing stories and items related to Chad, I allow Matthew and Connor to decide what we do on the special days of remembering—his birthday, death anniversary, and Father's Day. This choice allows them some control in how they celebrate and grieve him. They have chosen things like planting a bush that they decorate every November (my mom's clever idea), writing messages on balloons and letting them go, visiting his grave, volunteering at A Wider Circle, or taking a bike ride and having a picnic.

My friend Laura collaborates with her three children as to what to post on Facebook each birthday and Father's Day. This is one of their favorite things to do together in his memory. It not only honors him, allows them to freely say his name, and helps others remember him, but it also helps *them* remember him. The stories that people reply back with make them laugh and smile, and they keep his memory alive.

Practically speaking, one of the most important things to investigate for children after a parent dies are social security benefits, and/or military benefits if the deceased spouse was in the armed forces. Until they are eighteen years old, children of deceased parents can qualify for survivor benefits through social security, income that can help both the surviving children and spouse. I refer to other organizations that can help financially in the Additional Resources section at the end of this book.

In addition to securing financial wellness for our children, according to ChildrenGrieve.org:

> *Greater than any education, information, or advice we can give to children who are grieving is to allow them to connect with other children going through a similar experience. When children have the opportunity to interact with one another, they feel less alone.*[58]

There are a number of ways to help children make these connections.

I have been fortunate enough, I suppose I could say, to have friends whose children have also lost their fathers. It is helpful for my boys to be with these children. The one thing they long for, especially in these adolescent years, is to be just like everyone else. Being with children in similar situations to their own makes them feel normal.

I can remember an incident when a married friend and her children were visiting. Her young son innocently said to Matthew and Connor, "Well, you don't have a dad anymore."

Ugh.

I quickly interjected that they would *always* have a dad. He just didn't live here on this Earth anymore. With widows' children these things are understood. The absence of a parent is normal, and my children do not stand out.

Another way to help foster these types of relationships is through camps and grief groups.

---

58 "About Childhood Grief," The National Alliance for Grieving Children.

Free camps exist solely for the purpose of helping children heal from the loss or sickness of a parent and connect with other children in similar situations. I have listed several of these camps in the Additional Resources section at the back of this book along with a number of national organizations available to support grieving children and their parents.

A school-based program aiming to meet the goal of relating to other children is called Good Grief. Good Grief's charge is to "teach resiliency and facilitate healthy coping in the lives of more than nine hundred children each month by providing a caring and understanding environment that is like no other."[59] This is one of those places where our kids can feel normal.

My boys attended this group the year their father died. Matthew actually attended twice, as he switched schools and two students in his grade at his new school lost a parent when he arrived. It really benefitted them. Something to take into consideration, though, is that schools sometimes do not have enough students who have lost a parent to participate, so students who lost a grandparent or someone else important in their lives may attend as well. This is such a different type of loss, however. To me, mixing these groups minimizes the loss of a parent and diminishes the goal of helping children relate to other children. School counselors are able to answer questions about this program's availability at your school and who would participate.

---

59 "Compassion. Support. Community," Good Grief.

Another helpful group my children and I attended was a hospice bereavement group a few months after Chad died. Chad was not ever in hospice, but hospice offers free groups to any parents and children, free of charge.

In the group we attended, everyone ate pizza together to start the meeting. This was a nice time where we could chat, catch up on the day, and meet families whose parent had also died. Later, the children broke into similar-aged groups and made art projects and shared stories centered around healing. The parents migrated to an adjacent room with the other adults and two hospice counsellors. This time was so important because it helped us feel like we were normal too. In a room full of widows and widowers, I felt at home.

The emotional health of the surviving parent is critical to the healing of the child. The ability to maintain routines and allow children to express their grief in a safe home is paramount in the healing process. ChildrenGrieve.org states, "Research has shown that one of the top indicators of how well children will do after the death of a significant person in their life is directly related to the type of relationship they have with the surviving adult(s) in their lives and how well these adults are able to cope with their own grief."[60]

In the following section, I name several strategies that can help us as adults cope with grief. Our children's futures are so closely tied to our success in doing so.

---

60 "About Childhood Grief," The National Alliance for Grieving Children.

CHAPTER 11

THIS IS HARD

I have never felt worse pain, not even from the actual death of my husband, than shouldering my children's grief.

Some grief is easier to "parent" than others. The more difficult manifestations of grief in our children can make a life that already feels too difficult to handle one hundred times harder. On top of that, the world can be cruel to our children in their fragile state, which also adds an extra weight to parenthood.

When asked how their children are coping, all the widows whom I interviewed for this book start by explaining how their children are grieving differently from one another. "If I've seen one person in grief, I've only seen that one person in grief. I can't compare one griever to another," says David Kessler, the author of *Finding Meaning: The Sixth Stage of Grief.* This applies not only to us as adults, but also to kids.[61]

---

61 Elisabeth Kübler-Ross and David Kessler, *On Grief and Grieving*, 170.

My boys are different grievers. Connor is what Kessler calls a "practical griever." These are the people who don't grieve publicly and don't seem to grieve privately.[62] Connor rarely looks at his Daddy Box. He has a gong that Chad got in China displayed in his bedroom, and he used to pound it every now and again when he entered his room, but now it sits silent.

When I ask Connor if he misses his dad, he says, "No, barely ever." He will, however, cry randomly after someone accidentally eats his chicken finger. He seems to let sadness fill him up over time, like a teacup, until he can no longer hold it in, and the cup runneth over. This is a rare occurrence, and I don't believe that he even knows his tears are related to his ongoing grief. It simmers under the surface, unnamed and unnoticed, until it can't be contained anymore.

Kessler says these practical grievers are often misunderstood because, on the outside, it appears they don't care. They may even say that they don't care. But they do. They just carry the pain differently than others.[63]

On the other hand, Matthew outwardly expresses his sadness. He plays with the items in his Daddy Box. He puts some old clocks from Chad's office up around his room. He touches and reorganizes the pieces of clothing that he chose from Chad's closet. Then he puts them back away, along with his wish for his dad to be alive, for a time when another wave hits. Matthew sleeps with what he calls a good luck charm. It is a small, round, plastic souvenir that Chad bought at

---

62 David Kessler, *Finding Meaning: The Sixth Stage of Grief*, 31.

63 Ibid.

the Guinness factory when we were in Ireland, well before Matthew was born. The word "Guinness" is painted across the front, and the teeniest tiniest little bit of Guinness beer is sealed inside. This good luck charm resides inside Matthew's pillowcase, and he refuses to sleep without it.

My heart hurts more than I ever could have imagined for my children's loss. When Matthew cries and tells me he misses his dad, I cry right along with him. Not because I miss his dad, which I do, but because I want to take his pain and hold it for him. I can't heal that hole that will always be in his heart. Both boys have gone through therapy, and I even found Matthew a male therapist in order to offer him a positive male influence, but no one can take the place of a father once you have lost him.

Sometimes children's behavior markedly changes as a result of this hurt. Stacy Feintuch, in her *Widow Wears Pink* blog, writes about her daughter, Amanda, who seemed fine shortly after her father died. The family was Jewish, and Amanda was of age to be planning and attending many Bat Mitzvahs. She was busy. However, over the course of a year, Amanda began to withdraw. Her grades slipped, she wanted to be alone in her room, she seemed angry and quiet, and she was no longer the social girl she once was.

Amanda's dad had always been the one who understood her lowest points best. He was the patient one whom she could rely on to be level-headed and bring peace to the family. Feintuch says, "Suddenly, he wasn't there anymore. I think at some point this all hit her, and she didn't know how to handle it. Her way was to withdraw, and that was when she went dark."

After several misattempts at therapy, Stacy and her daughter found a wonderful therapist and a therapy group that made all the difference. Amanda is now doing well, after many tears and bumps along the road.[64]

Oftentimes our children's grief manifests as fear and anxiety, just as ours does. Elisabeth Kübler Ross and David Kessler, in their book *On Grief and Grieving*, say, "A child who experiences a death of a loved one loses her innocence quickly. She learns that life doesn't hold guarantees, and that makes her feel like she can't count on anything."[65]

Up to this year, Connor got upset whenever I told him that I was going out with friends. He always said, "You just left us," even though I made a practice of never leaving them for social purposes more than once a week. He hugged me four or five times before letting me go. He still does this whenever I leave him, even at bedtime.

One summer, when I became sick with Lyme disease, I could barely get out of bed. Connor's behavior was awful. My initial reaction was to get upset with him and punish him, until I realized this is how my practical griever deals with feelings that are too big for him. He shuts down. He began ignoring his grandparents and me.

---

64 Stacy Feintuch, "When my Daughter Went Dark."

65 Kübler-Ross, *On Grief and Grieving*, 170.

Finally, I had a private talk with him. I explained that I thought I understood he was worried about me. I explained that most times when people get sick, they get better. I was sick but I was not going to die like his dad. He hugged me tightly and cried. His behavior improved afterward. He didn't want to be rude and disrespectful, but when life gets to be too much, he goes into protection mode. Connor never knows when he might lose someone again, and his coping mechanism is to block off any feeling before he gets hurt.

This idea of anxiety due to loss can be exacerbated at certain times as well. During the COVID-19 pandemic, many widows talked about their children being even more worried about their remaining parent's well-being. With all the discussion of death caused by the virus, and a premature understanding of the fragility of life, it is no wonder why children who have lost a parent worry.

Lacey Bruno's son, Ricky, lost his dad when he was three. He is sixteen now, and Lacey is the only parent he has ever known. Since Ricky is in high school and fairly self-sufficient, Lacey forgot one day during the pandemic to tell him that she was running to the gym. Ricky arrived home to an empty house, and he became frantic. He began calling friends and family asking if they knew where Lacey was and if they had seen her.

When Lacey walked in the door a few hours later, Ricky was furious, "Where have you been? You have to tell me where you are going!" Lacey didn't realize that Ricky still worried about his only parent, his rock, not being there anymore.

Sometimes life gets hard for our kids because they are easy targets as they grapple with their new reality. Kelley Roger's son, David, was eleven when his dad went missing. His mom explained him as "a child of sunshine." He never had anything go wrong before in his life. He had just started middle school, which is typically a difficult transition for any child. He was no longer surrounded by the comfort of a small elementary school with the familiar faces of his teachers and peers. David was angry and confused, and he felt as if all eyes were on him as kids talked behind his back about how his father was missing.

When they found that his father had died, David struggled to connect with his old friends. Kelley says, "From an adult standpoint, that makes perfect sense. But from a kid standpoint, it just becomes more of a narrative of 'what's wrong with me,' and 'my life sucks because my dad died.'"

Most of David's peers were supportive and understood his suffering, but others, Kelley says, "just didn't want anything to do with him because he was grieving and that was weird. It made him unusual." A handful of kids even enjoyed using his weakness against him to push his buttons. "When you have a child who is of that age, fitting in and conformity all of a sudden become the most important things." Kids would mutter under their breath to him about not having a dad, and it would fill him with anger. He even broke his hand once trying to control his anger over something hurtful another student said about his dad.

Recently, David, now in high school, has made great strides in understanding that the world is not out to get him. "It takes a village to raise our children. And the village has been so good to my children, except the ones that weren't." Many times, Kelley needed to step in with the school and be David's advocate. She would tell David that he was in charge of his reactions to the other kids. "But at the same time," she said, "you have people kicking your kid in the teeth, and the mother bear in you wants to defend him." It's a dance we do between advocating for our children and teaching them to advocate for themselves.

With all the trauma and big feelings surrounding death, our instinct as moms is often to shield our kids from any outside harm, especially when the death of your child's father is new and raw.

I can remember the week when Matthew and Connor went back to first grade after Chad had died. I worked at their school, so the teachers and parents knew our family well and understood what my wishes would be on how I would like to handle their transition back.

Mrs. Traub, the counsellor, had met with each class and talked to them about how Connor and Matthew's dad had died and how they may be sad and need a friend. The teachers, who had all so graciously attended Chad's funeral, were in the ready position: ready to gather them in, embrace them, and shower love on them; ready to give them a routine that would help them feel like the world was normal again.

Being in that after-death daze, I don't even remember worrying about their re-entry. And the boys did not complain or put up a fight. Things seemed to go smoothly, until one day the principal called me. She was also my boss at the time, so I thought little of it.

"I'm sorry to call you, but there was an incident at lunch where one of the students was talking about Matthew's dad, and Matthew got upset and needed to go to the counselor."

My heart hurt a little extra for Matthew hearing that he was going through this, but I figured he would hear many people talk about his dad in the coming weeks. However, when he got home and told me the full story, my claws came out.

According to him, a bunch of boys were sitting at the lunch table, and one of them was asking Matthew if his dad died. One boy started laughing about it and making fun of him. Now, as a teacher and parent, I know that seven-year-old boys are typically clueless, especially when it comes to social situations and dealing with uncomfortable feelings. But this did not stop my blood from boiling, and a feeling of rage came from such a deep place that I wanted to scream.

Stacy Feintuch, in her *Widow Wears Pink* blog, tells of a similar feeling. Very shortly after her husband, Howie, died the power in the neighborhood went out for days. Stacy was forced to move out of her house with no heat and electricity into her friend's house that was unaffected and where other families had taken refuge as well.

While she and her girls were there, an incident involving her daughter, Amanda, and her friend's child occurred. One of Amanda's friends yelled at Stacy, telling her that Amanda needed to listen to whatever they were telling her to do, something that Amanda did not feel comfortable doing.

Amanda ran outside crying. Stacy found her sitting on the front steps in the cold crying and saying she wanted her dad. "I remember thinking to myself that this was as bad as it could get. This was rock bottom. These were truly the worst days. I was a homeless widow crying outside in the dark with my daughter. If I could have crawled into a hole at that moment and taken both of my girls with me, I would have."[66] I can many times over relate to that feeling.

Their pain is our pain. I often still wish I could remove my children from any feelings of hurt, hopelessness, or loneliness. I wish I could put them in a bubble filled with all the things they love and keep them there forever. But I can't, and I shouldn't.

For years now, Matthew has randomly said to me, "I wanna go home." I never knew what he meant because we were always home when he said it. For a while I thought he meant he wanted to go back to live in our old house where we had lived for the first five years of his life. I thought that maybe he related that house to the years when Chad was healthy.

Just this year I realized what he means when I saw the following meme on a young widow's repost on Twitter.

---

66 Feintuch, "The Worst Days."

"I am homesick for a place I am not sure even exists. One where my heart is full. My body loved. And my soul understood."[67]

It hit me like a brick when I read it. In his big twelve-year-old heart, where his ability to express himself has not yet caught up with the emotion he feels, Matthew is trying to say that he misses that feeling of completeness that having his dad in his life gave him.

To be honest, I wanna go home too.

---

67 Young Widow (@byyoungwidow), "Kinda wanting this again...#Widowhood," Twitter, July 13, 2020, 5:04 p.m.

CHAPTER 12

THE THINGS THAT DIDN'T HAPPEN

"The loss is felt in the things that didn't happen. It is the absence of a memory."

—LAURA KELLER

Laura Keller not only lost her husband, Joe, early, but she also lost her mother at a young age. Growing up, she missed her mother most during the important times in her life when she should have been there.

When Laura explained this idea to me, I couldn't stop the lyrics of the Cole Swindell song, "You Should Be Here," from replaying in my head.

It also reminded me of a quote that I had read before from an unknown author:

You were unsure which pain is worse—the shock of what happened or the ache for what never will.[68]

Even as an adult, I am pained by the absence of Chad. I find myself still counting out four plates when setting the table. I'm still taken aback each time I open the garage and his car is not there.

It is what no longer exists that is most painful. The lack. The lack of Chad's voice bellowing out, "HELLOOOOO!" when arriving home from a long day of work; the lack of never again seeing him unbutton the cuffs of his shirt and roll up his sleeves before carving the turkey. These images that have become a part of how I remember Chad will never be a part of my boys' memory.

As *One Fit Widow*, Michelle Steinke-Baumgard says of her children, "The pain of missing their father is nothing compared to the pain of knowing they will never understand firsthand his laugh, his giant bear hugs or his amazing heart."[69]

Graduations, weddings, the birth of a first child…my heart breaks for our children, that they will always have this chasm to cross every time they experience happiness. A shadow that will always lurk in the sunshine.

For her youngest child, Laura said Joe's absence was felt most when she made the softball team and Joe wasn't there to see it.

---

68 "Twenty-Seven Quotes to Help You Heal After Losing a Child."

69 Michelle Steinke-Baumgard, "Brown-Eyed Boy."

For her oldest, it was graduation from high school. "For me," Laura says, "it's that I actually miss him. The saddest thing for them is that we can't really understand their feelings. It is so hard not to be able to fix their grief. I wish I could say, 'Here's an ice cream cone. Now you will be okay.'"

Nicki Bunting and her boys feel this absence in the sport of football. Nicki says, "My dad died when I was six. So, I know what it's like to look around and see the guys with a dad."

Football, in particular, has been difficult for Nicki to swallow because of the nepotism that often exists between fathers and sons. "You know some of the positions that my kids want to play, that they're good enough to play, those positions are given to the coach's kid."

Nicki's husband, Bubba, was an athlete and a soldier, and he would have loved to coach his boys if he had lived. "I know one hundred percent if Bubba were here, he'd be coaching their football teams. And my kids would be able to play those positions."

Her boys feel it too. It pains them all being in this powerless position. "It's little tiny things like that which ingrain themselves into our everyday existence. They are just unfair to my kids, and I'm mad that someone would do this to our family."

When Cheryl Barnes, the author of the *Black Women Widows Empowered* blog, lost her husband Tony in 2014, she was left with two young boys to raise alone. From pregnancy, she and her husband had worried about raising their Black boys in today's society.

Tony had experienced racism in his life. Cheryl says he told her, "He would be here to teach our boys how to navigate life in America as a Black man. We expected that he would be there and guide his boys into Black manhood. I never expected to have to grieve not only his life but the loss of his wisdom. Wisdom that I honestly don't have."[70]

Like all widows, we try to be both mother and father to our children. Sometimes we are enough. However, much of the time, we cannot do justice to the way our husbands would have imparted wisdom to our children.

Barnes says:

> *I can tell them all about being Black in America, but I don't know the things their father knew. I can't tell them how he felt. I can't tell them how he dealt with any of it. I can't relay his fears for our boys to them. I can only imagine the dehumanizing feelings he had. He was a man, and yet he wasn't treated like one. He never wanted that for them. Deep in his soul, he wanted to protect them from all of that. I can try to do all of that as their mother, but what they need is their father to tell them what I can't. It is unfair to them that he can't.*[71]

Gena-mour Barrett authored an article entitled "Seven Things No One Tells You About Losing A Parent as A Child," where she describes how she felt when she lost her father when she was seven years old:

---

70 Cheryl Barnes, "#Grieving While Black."

71 Ibid.

The weight of my grief came to me in small doses at random stages of my life. It came when I sat in the back of my friend's car and listened to her chat with her dad about what they were going to eat for dinner. It came when I watched my classmates trail behind their mums and dads at parents' evening. It came on various Father's Days, when I'd joke smugly about not having to spend any money, and then wonder what it would be like if I actually had a dad to spend money on. It came, and it came, and it came. Each wave hit me just that little bit harder, until thirteen years after my dad's death, on the front pew at my grandfather's funeral, I began to cry. I cried for every moment my father and I never had and never will have, and I finally understood how dreadful it actually was.[72]

Others have graciously stepped in over time in my life to fill in the gaps and make things feel less dreadful for my children.

For instance, my dad takes the boys fishing and helps them put together LEGOs and drones. Chad's dad teaches them how to be archers and play Rummikub.

Heather Hofmann started a tradition with her father-in-law who lives in Germany. He engages in a cooking class with her boys on weekends in an effort to give them male experiences. Each week, he sends Heather a recipe so she can shop for the ingredients. Then, Finn and Grayson follow Opa's lead as they cook a meal together over Zoom.

---

72 Gena-mour Barrett, "Seven Things No One Tells You About Losing A Parent as A Child."

I can remember when Matthew first started playing basketball two months after Chad died. I could not bear to think of him playing a sport, with all his future successes and failures, without his dad there to watch. One night he was crying, and I asked him what was wrong. He told me, "All the other kids have their dads there." Right in the gut.

That night, I called Chad's friend Mindy, who had offered up her husband Steve if I ever needed help with the boys. He had coached his daughter's basketball teams, so I figured he would fill Chad's shoes perfectly. Steve was more than willing to help.

It turned out that having him there didn't help Matthew at all though. Steve cheered for him, praised him after each practice, gave him pointers, but it wasn't what Matthew needed.

What Matthew needed was his dad.

In my early days of widowhood, I thought that having a man present would solve all our problems. Eventually, though, I learned that some problems are unsolvable. I am beyond thankful for Steve and all the men who continue to step in to fill these gaps. My boys need the company of good male role models. However, as important as these relationships are, they will never settle that feeling in Matthew and Connor's gut that something is missing. It always will be.

Matthew and Connor's dad will never be here to watch them play sports again. He will never be here to see them accepted into their favorite colleges or fall in love for the first time. Never will he tell them how proud he is on their wedding days. He will be forever thirty-nine-years-old, and my children's experience of their dad will stop there. There will always be the things that didn't happen. And the absence of what might have been aches.

CHAPTER 13

WILL THEY BE OKAY?

For three years, every month mid-cycle, I would visit the fertility clinic daily for an internal ultrasound and blood work in an attempt to make a baby. I would inject myself with hormones and medicines and pray that my numbers looked good at the end of the month, indicating that I was pregnant.

For a couple of years, I would cry at the end of every cycle for the life that still had not been created. We took breaks and had good numbers at the end of a month, only for them to fall a few days later. Eventually, Chad and I decided to do IVF, or In Vitro Fertilization. IVF is an intense process of growing and harvesting eggs from the mother and fertilizing them with sperm from the father. After viable embryos emerge, fertility specialists place them back into the woman's womb to see if they will grow in that environment.

The first time, it did not work and was heartbreaking for both of us. The second time it did, with another loss of pregnancy to follow—doubly heartbreaking. The third time gifted us with the two lives that continue to bring me joy to this day.

The struggle of infertility helped prepare me for my husband being sick and dying.

It readied me in a number of ways. One, it taught me that no matter how much we hope and pray, we cannot control every aspect of our lives. As a mentor of mine used to say, "We plan, and God laughs." Up until that point in my life, everything had run in a routine, systematic, somewhat controlled way. Not being able to have a child when I snapped my fingers was the first time I realized my will mattered little in certain life plans.

Infertility taught me that despite extreme sadness and continued loss, I was resilient. I could lose one unviable pregnancy, pass another month with no success, and hop back up into the saddle once my body had healed. I could go through the uncomfortable motions time and time again because I had the grit to do it. Through that painful chapter in my life, I found my strength. I learned to rise again when the world brought me to my knees.

Many adults have had experiences like this that have defined, strengthened, and calloused them as adults. Breakups, the loss of a parent or close friend, loved ones moving far away—these losses equip us to handle some amount of trauma and grief. Our children, God willing, have not had the types of repeated disappointments and losses.

When my children's father died, they had no strategies up their sleeves for dealing with grief. They had never needed any. So, I worried.

Will they be okay?

I was terrified they wouldn't be able to succeed in life without a father to guide them toward being a man. Would the trauma and grief they have experienced impede their ability to find joy and fulfillment in life? Would it create tendencies in them to turn to drugs, alcohol, or other forms of addiction to quiet their pain?

I have read how a disproportionate number of men and women in prison have lost a parent at an early age. It is easy for a child to go astray, especially a boy without a positive male role model in his life. I reminded myself that many boys have male role models, and they are not positive. Many children are growing up in families with no mom or dad for reasons other than death. Many children have families who are divided by divorce. And many of these boys transition into contributing members of society.

My boys are not alone in struggle, but this did not ease my fears.

One day, a friend told me about Malcolm Gladwell's book, *David and Goliath.* Gladwell, a Canadian journalist, columnist for *The New Yorker*, and author of a number of best-selling books, wrote this book based upon the premise that suffering and disadvantage are often viewed as negative, but they may very well lead to advantages in life. He calls this the "Theory of Desirable Difficulty." I had to read it.[73]

---

73 Malcolm Gladwell, *David and Goliath*, 97.

In his book, Gladwell cites a study done by Marvin Eisenstadt in the 1960s. Eisenstadt studied the *Encyclopedia Britannica* and *Encyclopedia Americana* searching for individuals whose biography covered more than one column, meaning they were famous enough to have earned that much print on the page. After ten years of study, looking at the profiles of each of the people whom he found meeting this criterion, he discovered something stunning. "A quarter had lost at least one parent before the age of ten. By age fifteen, 34.5 percent had at least one parent die."[74]

A historian named Lucille Iremonger was researching British prime ministers around the same time. She found, in the group of prime ministers whom she studied, that 77 percent of them had lost a parent before their sixteenth birthday. This was double the number of children who lost their parents during that period, in that location, in that same socioeconomic group.

In addition, Gladwell points out that twelve presidents, from Washington to Obama, lost fathers at a young age. That is almost one-third of our US presidents.[75]

Gladwell calls these individuals "eminent orphans," and he surmises that what they gained from losing their parent was "acquired courage." "What happens," he wonders, "to children whose worst fear is realized—and then they discover

74 Ibid., 141.

75 Ibid., 142.

they are still standing? Couldn't they also gain...a self-confidence that is the very father and mother of courage?"[76]

He goes on to tell, "If you take away a mother or a father, you cause suffering and despair, but one time in ten out of that despair rises an indomitable force."[77] One in ten children who have lost a parent become incredibly successful in their various fields of employment. If these children can rise again after the worst imaginable thing that could happen to them actually did, they can doubtlessly rise up from anything that knocks them down.

Malcolm Gladwell's words gave me hope for my children's financial and professional futures, despite their early loss. However, these types of achievements are only a small piece of their well-being. My goals for my children have less to do with making a ton a money and more to do with being good people, good fathers, good husbands, being content, and living meaningful lives.

According to the National Alliance for Grieving Children, children can experience personal growth, the kind that can lead one to being a good and whole person, as a result of grief. Some of the ways in which children may grow is that they may become more compassionate, they may value relationships more, or they may appreciate life more. These areas of growth mirror the types of post-traumatic growth that adults also encounter, mentioned in Chapter 2. The National Alliance for Grieving Children does point out that "personal

---

76 Ibid., 153.

77 Ibid., 275.

growth does not diminish the sense of loss or grief a person feels, nor does it imply that someone's death was a positive experience."[78] It simply means that strength and wisdom can come from struggle.

Brené Brown, a research professor who studies courage, vulnerability, shame, and empathy, recently gave a virtual commencement speech to the graduates at her University of Texas alma mater. She spoke of this same concept.

Brown said:

> *Your ability to live a life that's full of love and meaning, to make the world a braver and kinder place, to disrupt and reshape the future, has very little to do with the greatness of your plan. It depends completely on your ability to get back up and begin again when your plan fails...the exact same number of times that you fall, trip, and get pushed down.*[79]

She continues, "I've never seen a single person who's built a life, a family, or a career, that did not have to scratch their way out from a fall and begin again a hundred times."[80]

I learned this in my thirties. My boys, I pray, learned it when they were seven.

---

78 "About Childhood Grief," National Alliance for Grieving Children.

79 Brené Brown, "Don't Be Afraid to Fall," video, 2:00.

80 Ibid., 13:34.

SECTION IV.

SAFE HARBOR

"The reality is that you will grieve forever. You will not 'get over' the loss of a loved one; you will learn to live with it. You will heal and you will rebuild yourself around the loss you have suffered. You will be whole again, but you will never be the same. Nor should you be the same, nor would you want to."

~ELISABETH KÜBLER-ROSS, *ON GRIEF AND GRIEVING*

CHAPTER 14

RELATIONSHIPS WITH THE DEAD

Elisabeth Kübler-Ross and David Kessler, in their book *On Grief and Grieving*, note that "in a strange way, as we move through grief, healing brings us closer to the person we loved. A new relationship begins."[81]

This word "relationship" sounded strange to me the first time I saw it used in this context. A relationship, to me, was a bond between living beings, not a dead person and a living person. However, as I thought about some of the ways that I continued to connect with Chad, I realized that "relationship" was actually the perfect word for this phenomenon.

In their article entitled "Processes of Grieving: How Bonds Are Continued," Dennis Klass and Tony Walters surmise that people maintain bonds, or relationships, with the deceased in four ways:

81 Elisabeth Kübler-Ross and David Kessler, *On Grief*, 25.

1. Sensing the deceased's presence
2. Talking to the dead
3. Using the deceased as a moral guide
4. Talking about the deceased[82]

These may sound strange; they did to me. Now, though, these bonds are commonplace in not only my life, but also many other widows' lives.

The moment Chad died, I felt his presence in the room. I sat with him until I knew that no life was left in his corpse. His body clearly was now an empty vessel, no movement or warmth anymore. However, I felt his spirit as if he were sitting beside me, embracing me. There was an overwhelming feeling of calm and peace inside of me that seemed to come from nowhere and everywhere all at once. He was vividly present.

When my friend Heather's husband, Ralf, died in their home, Heather also felt this presence. "His soul passed right through me," she swears.

In his book *Finding Meaning: The Sixth Stage of Grief*, David Kessler asserts that "80 percent of bereaved people say that they have felt a loved one's presence at some point after they died. Many times, it occurs around one of our senses." Like the smell of a cologne, laughter that is unmistakably theirs, or the way a spring breeze gently caresses your face as it rustles the leaves—we feel them with us at those moments.[83]

---

82 Elizabeth A. Doughty et al., *Current Trends in Grief Counseling*, 3.

83 David Kessler, *Finding Meaning: The Sixth Stage of Grief*, 224.

Oftentimes, this feeling of presence happens long after the actual moment of death. After about a year of holding onto her husband Jon's ashes, Melanie Green decided to plant a tree in her yard and spread them there. "I feel him when I go down there. It's cheesy, but I usually hold the tree branch, like I'm holding his hand or something." This tree is where Melanie maintains her relationship with Jon.

Elisabeth Kübler Ross says, "If you feel your loved one's presence, do not doubt it. They still exist." Whatever your religious beliefs and ideas of what happens to a person following death might be, I have found some reassurance in believing that the deceased do still exist in some form when their bodies no longer house their souls.

I engage in the other three types of bonding as well. I do talk to and about Chad. In instances where I wish I had his guidance I wonder what he would have thought or done. "What would (insert deceased partner's name here) do?" is a question that recurred in many of the interviews I conducted, literature I read, and podcasts to which I listened. Every time someone mentions the idea, I am reminded of the bracelets that people used to wear (maybe some still do) emblazoned with the letters WWJD—What Would Jesus Do? Those bracelets, popular in the 1990s, were worn by Christians who desired to be reminded of their moral compass when making decisions.

For me, Chad provided that moral compass. We bounced ideas off each other. As a team, we became who we ethically and morally were destined to be. I looked to him to measure how strongly I felt about certain issues. He was my sounding board.

So, it makes sense that in death, as in life, I wonder, *What would he think or do*? What would he think about the 2020 election results? What would he have done in this pandemic when we were all forced to spend so much time together? What would he think about the kids being allowed to play Call of Duty? I wish I knew.

Or, like my friend Andrea Albanese has come to understand, even if we do know what our spouses would have done when they were alive, life is different now. We have to do what is right for us.

Andrea has five children, and her husband Jim asked her to go back to work when he was sick because he wanted to make sure the family would have adequate health care. Jim had always been the sole provider, and after a year on long-term disability, their health care had come to a halt. Andrea says:

> *You're just going forward because you don't have a choice, and you do things that you never thought he would want you to do. He had no idea what this life was going to look like for me. How I will be with my children twenty-four seven during the pandemic. He didn't know what it now takes to survive together. He thought I needed to work, and I just assumed that I was carrying out his wishes by working. But it was killing me.*

Andrea eventually quit her job after consulting a financial advisor. For the foreseeable future, she is happy to be a stay-at-home-mom, but not without some guilt and wondering WWJD.

In addition to Klass and Walters's four bonds, I would add one more. People may call this coincidence (or call me certifiable), but I truly believe that if a person has an open mind, she may catch a glimpse of signs from the deceased.

The week after Chad passed, many things happened that, looking back, I am thankful I was open to noticing.

First, the day after his death, my best friend (and one of Chad's best friend's too) Heather showed up at our door unexpected. I was shocked to see her. Not only had she driven an hour to get to my house without my knowledge (she is not the spontaneous type), but also when I greeted her, she and I were wearing the exact same gray and white, block-patterned three-quarter length shirt. I had owned it for years, and I didn't wear it often because that type of sleeve always makes me feel drafty, especially in November. I think I probably hadn't done laundry in weeks, and it was the only thing left in my closet that was clean. We laughed at the coincidence.

Not a week later, Chad's family flew in from Texas for the funeral. Chad's brother, Shawn, and his family filed into the house with hugs and condolences. As Shawn's seventeen-year-old son, Trevor, removed his coat, I could see what he was wearing. I had to do a double take. It was the same Tommy Hilfiger sweater that Chad had purchased immediately after college some twenty years prior. The sweater was unique, navy blue with red trim around the neck and yellow trim around the cuffs. I tried to wrack my brain. Did Chad give Trevor that sweater during a previous visit to Texas? That was impossible because I had recently seen it in his closet. I asked Trevor where he had purchased it. It turned out that he found it in a thrift shop earlier that month and liked it so much he had to have it. *Hmm.* Maybe not a coincidence. Maybe Chad was sending us a sign.

These signs continue today. The changing numbers on my clock are a good example. Without me touching it at all, the red digital numerals tune into a specific radio station. The numbers on the clock regularly tell the time, but without warning, all of a sudden, they flip: 89.5, 89.5, 89.5.

Sometimes they flip to 89.4. I believe that is Drew, our friend who died the year before Chad. I'm not sure I believe in numerology. I have never actually had to think much about it in my past, but this repeated occurrence led me to investigate the importance of these numbers. What I read is that "Angel Number Eighty-Nine comes as a reminder to stay focused on your goals and carry your projects and enterprises out to the end. When we stay focused on our goals and positive outcomes, we attract the exact conditions that we need to achieve them."[84] This could apply to anything, but it comforts me to think that Chad and Drew are watching over me and rooting for me to accomplish all I set forth to do.

Melanie Green's husband was a police officer. She said that the summer he died, blue butterflies surrounded her in the yard of her home and everywhere she went. I, of course, immediately looked up what blue butterflies symbolized

---

84 "Angel Number 89," TSOT.

(aside from the obvious blue being the color of the police force). Everything I found alluded to blue butterflies being a symbol of the spirit embracing change and transformation.

Elisabeth Kübler-Ross tells of the butterflies carved into the walls of the concentration camps during World War II. She says, "They are an enduring symbol of transformation, that even in the face of great loss we will continue, someway, somehow." She goes on to say, "In grief, just like in death, there is a transformation for the living. If you do not take the time to grieve, you cannot find a future in which loss is remembered and honored without pain."[85]

In her *Badass Widow* blog, Mary Kate Tischler tells a story of her two-year-old daughter seeing butterflies after her father died. Following his death, Mary Kate and her daughter traveled to Upstate New York several times to visit colleges with her stepson.

Multiple times on these trips, Mary Kate's daughter would say, "Butterflies, butterflies," as she pointed to a plain white indoor ceiling. Mary Kate googled this phenomenon, and she found this written by John Harricharan:

The caterpillar dies so the butterfly could be born. And, yet, the caterpillar lives in the butterfly and they are but one. So, when I die, it will be that I have been transformed from the caterpillar of earth to the butterfly of the universe.[86]

---

85 Kübler-Ross, *On Grief*, 207.

86 Mary Kate Tischler, "'Do you see the butterflies circling my head?'"

These butterfly sightings happened again and again for Mary Kate's daughter, always inside where there were no butterflies to be seen. Tischler says:

> *What makes this occurrence even stranger is that, while roaming around in an old Italian neighborhood in Philly that weekend, we came across a daycare center that had cutouts of all different kinds of animals, birds, and flowers in the windows. As we pointed to each thing, my daughter would identify it (yellow duck, red bird, etc.), but, when we'd point to one of the many butterflies on the window, she could not identify it. In other words, the only time that the word "butterfly" was in her vocabulary was when she was seeing ones that nobody else could see.*[87]

Her daughter was the recipient of a gift from her father. "Every time we went on a trip in those first few months after he died, he let us know that he was there with us by appearing for our daughter in the form of a butterfly. Maybe that sounds crazy to you, but I've never known anything to be more true."[88]

Most widows I spoke to had a story about their loved one sending them a sign in one form or another.

Charity Yanishak DeNeal noticed a string of signs from her late husband, Drew, one fall when she drove from Roanoke, Virginia, to Northern Virginia for their daughter's dance

---

87 Ibid.

88 Ibid.

competition. From Highway 66, Siri gave her directions to leave the highway at the wrong exit.

Charity did not know where she was. She thought she was lost. As she looked around, she recognized certain landmarks. Charity realized that she was right next to the apartment complex where Drew had lived immediately after graduating college. The area had changed with so much new construction in the past twenty-plus years that she had hardly recognized it. As she pulled over to the side of the road to figure out how to get back on the correct path, a massive semi-truck pulled up beside her. Written on the side of the truck was, "Drew Transport."

For Melanie Green's husband, Jon, music was a large part of his life. He played the guitar and had tons of albums stored on Google Play. Melanie has set up her Google Play so that after one CD ends, the music stops. Melanie must choose another album to play. There is never a continuous stream where the next CD starts to play automatically. There is no randomness, only music played by selection.

On their daughter Ainsley's birthday, after both of her children had gone to bed, Melanie was in the kitchen washing dishes and cleaning up after a fun day. That night, just after midnight when the album that Melanie was listening to finished, there was silence as usual. A split second later, a new song came on, but not from the previous album.

It was one of Jon's favorite songs, "Life by the Drop." They had played this song at his celebration of life. Melanie stood in the kitchen dumbstruck as she listened. Following that, the Black

Keys song "Girl Is on My Mind" came on, one of Melanie's favorites. Two individual signs from two different albums!

Believing in signs, Melanie's first thought was that they were meant for her, and she was on his mind. And then she remembered it was Ainsley's birthday. After that, no more music. Silence. This had never happened before, and it has never happened to her since. Chills.

A similar story about signs had to do with Nicki Bunting and her husband's dog tags. When Nicki got Bubba's dog tags back after he died, there was a curved dent in one of them. She knew that he had been wearing them that fateful day, as always, next to his chest. From time to time, Nicki would find herself examining them, wondering what could have caused that dent.

One day, a couple of years later during the closing on her new home, Nicki figured it out. Nicki held Bubba's dog tags as she signed the papers. "It made me feel really close to him because he was wearing those when he died." As she was fidgeting, moving her pen back and forth against them, the pen stopped in the groove. "The pen fit perfectly in that groove, and I remembered he used to clip a pen right under his shirt under his uniform." Nicki took this as a signal that he was there with her. Even though Nicki did not originally believe in signs, Bubba has since converted her into a believer.

In order to make sense of all that I was learning about death, grief, and life, I went to a medium this past summer—not something that I normally do. He said that all these things I call "signs" are actually the calling cards of the deceased;

the way that they let us know they are still here. I could go on and on about the signs I have felt that Chad has sent: cardinals, squirrels, woodpeckers knocking on windows, twin rainbows.

I love that he sends them and continues to inform us that he is present in some way, still, in our lives. When my sons see a beautiful sunset, they say, "Look mom! Look what Dad sent us." This relationship we have with Chad will continue to help us through the hardest times when we feel most alone.

About connections to the dead, Elisabeth Kübler-Ross shares, "If someone says they have experienced it, the only question that is important is, 'Were you comforted?'"[89] Whether you think this is crazy or not, the point is just that—if you do experience these bonds, allow yourself to gather peace from them. How lovely if our spouses truly are bestowing these gifts upon us.

89 Kübler-Ross, *On Grief*, 110.

CHAPTER 15

CONNECTION

Unlike SpongeBob, who my son Matthew tells me lives in a bubble (though I think he might be confused because I am fairly certain he lives in a pineapple), we live in a multifaceted, multicultural world. From the very beginning of this journey through loss, I have looked at people's lives around the globe. I am thankful for all that I have; I try not to focus on what I no longer do.

I would watch news programs with weeping widows holding their husbands who had been killed in bombings in war-torn countries. These same women lacked food or blankets for themselves or for their children. Images of children sleeping on the cold, bare earth, with no creature comforts after experiencing great trauma and loss. I would be so thankful for my personal situation. I would be grateful that I was not them.

This is what Elisabeth Kübler-Ross would call "comparing losses." In general, this practice is unhealthy, as Kübler-Ross explains, "Losses are very personal and comparisons never apply. No loss counts more than another. It is your loss that counts for you."[90]

I have had many conversations with friends about which is more difficult, your husband dying immediately in an accident or after having six years of life with him where he never felt well and was in-and-out of hospitals. I have also debated the idea of which is worse, divorce or death of a spouse.

This act of comparison actually sometimes helps me practice gratitude. If I feel pain for another person, I feel less for myself.

My friend Heather Hofmann who lost her husband, Ralf, only two years prior to the coronavirus pandemic felt this way. Her friend's husband died from the virus in the midst of the global shutdown. Because health officials did not want the virus to spread, his wife was unable to be by his side. He died alone. Groups were not permitted to gather, so she could only have a small celebration of his life.

After the funeral, Heather shared with me the relief of her own situation. "Thank God I had a chance to say goodbye to Ralf. I feel so lucky. At what point in my life did I start comparing death stories?"

Sharing stories and talking about loss are helpful for many people. In a book entitled *Writing to Heal,* a social psychologist and professor at University of Texas at Austin, Dr. James Pennebaker, asserts that "people who engage in expressive

---

90 Elisabeth Kübler-Ross and David Kessler, *On Grief*, 30.

writing report feeling happier and less negative than before writing."[91]

Similarly, "reports of depressive symptoms, rumination, and general anxiety tend to drop in the weeks and months after writing about emotional upheavals." People who kept their pain and struggles a secret died at higher rates. However, sharing their pain, even just by writing it down, had a positive effect on their health.[92]

Much literature exists about the healing effects of journaling. Elisabeth Kübler-Ross explains that writing "externalizes what is in us." She views it as a place where people may "deposit their feelings without worrying about someone else's reactions."[93]

In the grief group that I attended a few months after Chad died, one of our assignments was to write a letter to our deceased person. I put it off until the night before our session because I thought it was a little odd. When I finally snuggled into my warm bed with my pen and journal in hand, the words came slowly.

Soon, though, I was writing so quickly that my hand was aching. I hadn't realized how much I still needed to say to Chad. It was as if I were speaking to him through the words on the page. For the first night in months, I slept like a baby.

---

91 Brad Waters, "The New 10 Traits of Emotionally Resilient People."

92 Ibid.

93 Kübler-Ross, *On Grief*, 144.

For some, it may be sharing feelings and stories of loved ones in a journal. Others may find comfort in connecting with friends and family. Pastors or other religious leaders can fulfill this need as well. For me, it was all the above, along with my therapist.

In various cultures and generations, therapy is seen as a weakness; something only for the mentally ill. I wish such a stigma did not exist. Therapy, for me, was a life saver. How often do we get to sit for an hour and speak only about ourselves, without the shackles of the social construct of listen and respond?

My therapist, Mitra, taught me the art of listening to my body and breathing. She taught me to make a place for things on the calendar so that I was not constantly ruminating over what to do next. She taught me the gift of gratitude.

I have always been a bit superstitious. Since childhood, I would make a certain number of wishes when the clock turned a particular time (i.e., five wishes at 5:55). Mitra taught me to turn the idea of wishing for something into the practice of being grateful for something. Now, instead of making three wishes at 3:33, I inventory all that I am grateful for, and I name three of them. My gratefuls usually revolve around the health and safety of myself, my sons, my family, and friends. Sometimes I am just grateful for a good meal, warm weather, or food security.

In Jennifer Garman's book, *Flourish*, she explains how "gratitude helps magnify your positive emotions so you're more likely to adapt to the good things happening in your life. Additionally, gratitude helps you counteract negative emotions like resentment, regret, and envy." She cites a study out of the UCLA Mindfulness Awareness Research Center where they found that expressing gratitude actually changes the structure of the brain to make us happier and even healthier.[94]

Brené Brown says, "For twelve years of research, I have never heard a single person who talks about the capacity to really experience and soften into joy who does not actively practice gratitude."[95]

Most of us have the capacity to overcome debilitating grief, but many of us need help filling our toolbox with strategies like these. I went on a date with a man named Jim who had lost his son when he was an infant. He was lost in a spiral of blaming himself and being mad at the world. Jim would not consider therapy because he did not believe in its healing power until a colleague put him in touch with a male therapist named Paul. Jim said, "Paul helped me adapt ideas that were common sense that I already knew. He was like a tour guide." Paul didn't solve Jim's problems (irrational anger and anxiety). Rather, he helped him reframe his thinking and led him toward the strategies and tools (some new and some existing) to help make him whole again.

My friend Melanie says, "I feel like I should have graduated by now," but her sessions with her therapist bring her such

---

94 Jennifer Garman, *Flourish*, 26.

95 Brené Brown, "Dr. Brené Brown on Joy."

peace, and she relies on her feedback. She doesn't want to stop, nor should she feel pressure to.

One reason it is so comforting to speak to a therapist is because of a practice in our society known as the "mum effect." Sheryl Sandburg mentions in her book, *Option B*, that the "mum effect" is the idea that the majority of people avoid topics of conversation that are disturbing or sad.[96] We can all remember conversations after our husbands died when people did not even mention his name or the fact that he was dead. They spoke as if nothing had changed. This is not only awkward, but also painful to think that just being who you are causes someone such discomfort.

In her *One Fit Widow* blog, widow Michelle Steinke-Baumgard urges women to speak their husbands' names. "Saying his name is part of what heals me, makes me smile and gives me the gift of sweet memories. Saying his name teaches his children that he mattered in my life, your life, and more importantly, in their little lives. Saying his name brings his light back to the world."[97]

Sandburg explains how psychologists call the people who do openly speak of and ask questions about the deceased "openers." These people want to know how we are feeling and thinking. She mentions how these people are not necessarily our best friends, but they often have suffered through something themselves.[98]

---

96 Sheryl Sandberg and Adam Grant, *Option B*, 34.

97 Michelle Steinke-Baumgard, "Say Their Name."

98 Sandberg, *Option B*, 34.

This makes me reflect upon the friends whom I have made since Chad's passing. Most of them are openers. I have little time or patience for the closers.

My friend Lydia comes to mind as the greatest opener I have ever known. Lydia was a teenager when she lost her father in a plane crash. When Chad died, she and I were more acquaintances than friends. Our commonalities seemed to be limited to the fact that our children were in the same grade at school and we both had twins.

Throughout the past five years, Lydia has been there for me through all my ups and downs. Her powers of intuition are astounding. She will call me on my worst days without even knowing my day had been bad. She recorded all the important dates in my life: my birthday, Chad's birthday, the boys' birthday, my anniversary. For years, for each and every one of these benchmarks, she either sent me flowers, bought me chocolates, or just stopped by. Oftentimes, Lydia would include other friends' names on the various cards and gifts, but hers was always there.

My boys loved it when Lydia and her children would come around because they would bring them "taste tests." Sometimes these would be three different types of newfangled Pringles potato chip flavors. Other times, it would be multiple types of jellybeans. These taste tests lit our hearts for short periods of time during the dimmest days of our lives. Lydia helped me survive those first couple of years, and she helped me remember what it was to smile. In retrospect, Lydia is the one person who influenced me in seeing grief as more of a gift than a curse. Her experience as a young woman gave her the capacity to pay forward her wisdom and kindness and teach my family grace.

There are so many who have saved and continue to save me during the difficult times. I hope they all know how much I appreciate them.

- My mom and dad, who have come monthly to visit and to help me with the house and kids for the past five years. My mom texts me every single morning without fail, just to make sure I am safe and alive since I no longer have another adult to do that for me.

- My friends Heather, Karen, and Thalia, who make sure that I survive the saddest dates and that my yearly birthday winery and karaoke night always get planned. And Margie, whose mantra is "Chad guides me" whenever she delivers beautiful bouquets of flowers to my door.

- My friends Jamie and Jeff, who came to my house the first holiday after Chad died so that we didn't feel alone. They also come every summer to do fun things, like camp out with the boys.

The list goes on and on and on. My village is the reason that, five years later, my boys and I made it through. They are the reason we thrive.

Debbie Weiss, an introverted widow who writes a blog called *The Hungover Widow*, notes how difficult making these connections can be if they didn't already exist before a spouse's death. She found it less daunting to join classes and organizations that held her interest versus simply looking for people to befriend.[99]

She says:

> *It can be hard to "put yourself out there." But joining a gym or trying a painting class doesn't have to be. You're just doing something you already like (or in the case of the gym, need to do). I initially joined a yoga studio to deal with my anxiety, but I found a lovely group of women who included me in their activities. After I found my tribe, I began to feel grateful again for the first time since being widowed.*[100]

Another group easy to find commonalities with are fellow widows. I could not have survived those first few years after Chad passed away without my amazing tribe of strong, beautiful, and amazing widow friends. It is cathartic to share fears, laughter, stories, and worries with someone who completely understands every angle of your life. When this can no longer be your spouse, widow friends are the next best option.

Laura Keller, whom I quote often in this book, was in my hospice grief group about six months after we lost Chad. About that group, Laura said, "It was important for me to know that there were other people out there, people who I could share my story with."

---

99 Debbie Weiss, "Using a Beginner's Mind to Cope with the Loneliness of Widowhood."

100 Ibid.

Laura was that person for me in that group. She and I had quite a bit in common. We both had school-aged children, had husbands who died of cancer, and worked in the school system. We also had a common sense of humor and level-headedness. I don't get to see Laura often, but having her to bounce ideas off and to listen to her viewpoints has been mind-opening for me.

Since meeting Laura, I have accumulated a vast network of widow friends. They are some of my favorite people. They are all as different as snowflakes and fingerprints, but each one brings me a feeling of peace and solidarity that I feel with no one else.

If you don't know other young widows yet, not to worry! There are many ways to make this connection.

The hospice group I mentioned was free through our local hospice organization. There are other groups like this, for widows and widowers only, sponsored by churches, the military, and other organizations.

Lacey Bruno laughed when telling me about the church she belonged to when her husband died. They offered a bereavement group for widows at 10 a.m. on Thursdays. Unfortunately, as a working mother, she could never attend. But she also made the point that she would not have fit in anyway. Because many young widows have jobs, children, and many years ahead of them, the challenges are different. "You just can't lump us into that totally different category. Some of them had been married for thirty years. Totally different struggle," Lacey says. It truly is.

I was fortunate that most of the women in my group were young. The facilitators likely planned it that way. However, if the group had not been designed for young widows, it would have served me well to find one that was. We will never find our exact grief doppelgänger, someone who can relate to everything that we are feeling and experiencing, but we certainly have a better chance of connecting with those who understand our struggles in a group of similarly aged peers.

During the Covid-19 Pandemic, women losing their husbands lacked the ability to create these connections. In a NextAvenue.org article by Kevyn Burger, a young widow named Simone Andrews describes her experience when her forty-six-year-old healthy husband, LT, died from COVID.[101]

For the nineteen days he was sick the family could only connect via iPad. They did not know that he was going to die when he did, so they never even had a chance to say goodbye. They never again physically touched him.[102]

"We went into our grief bubble," Simone said. "My parents and in-laws couldn't come to be with us. It was too risky to see anyone. It's like we were marooned." On the same day that LT died, 876 others died in New York. Simone was not alone in her grief—she was simply isolated.[103]

---

101 Kevyn Burger, "'Not a Single Casserole'—What It's Like to Be Widowed by COVID-19."

102 Ibid.

103 Ibid.

Michelle Neff Hernandez, a widow and founder of Soaring Spirits International, a nonprofit that helps widows and widowers by holding events called Camp Widow across North America, saw these women in need of connection. In response, Neff Hernandez initiated Zoom meetings to bring these men and women who had lost their spouses to COVID together and give them the network they so desperately needed. Although they are not physically in the same space, these individuals are able to share their stories with others who are emotionally in the same space.

Hernandez says, "Grief naturally isolates you, but many of these widowed people have not touched anyone for months. That lack of affection and connection as this crisis has stretched on and on keeps them in that cauldron of pain."[104]

Another lifeline that allows widows to connect virtually is Facebook. Facebook has a handful of groups that focus particularly on young widows. To access them, all you do is go into "Groups" on Facebook and search, "Young Widows."

These groups are filled with widows, sometimes very young, who are going through struggles just like ours. I find myself tearing up at what some single women (and men) are enduring daily. The best part about these groups is that anytime anyone posts anything, many well-wishers who have been there too will react. The members prop you up. I needed to be cognizant that it is easy to go down a rabbit hole in these groups, but it is nice to know I will always be listened to and understood by real people on the other end of the chat.

---

104 Ibid.

Blogs are another digital support that many young widows whom I interviewed rely upon. Some blogs are associated with a website, and many of the websites contain resources for widows, like books to read and other blogs to follow. Some even offer courses where a live instructor or life coach will support you. Below is a list of my personal favorites:

Modern Widows Club
One Fit Widow
Black Women Widows Empowered
Badass Widow
DC Widow
Widow Wears Pink
Hot Young Widows Club
The Hungover Widow

Whether through journaling, interacting with friends and family, or fostering new relationships, connections can be a young widow's lifeline. I have embraced any and all that I found helpful and that worked for me logistically. It is no secret that we young widows have very little excess time or energy to spend. However, each and every time I have allowed myself space and time to commune with others and with myself, I have moved a tiny step closer to that feeling of wholeness that I seek.

CHAPTER 16

HELP OTHERS, HELP YOURSELF

"If you want to feel better, go help someone. You don't have to help a lot of people. Just do it once. You'll see. You'll do it again."

In his book, *Finding Meaning: The Sixth Stage of Grief,* David Kessler shares this anecdote from a father who lost his son in the terrorist attacks on 9/11. This father, Peter Alderman, and his wife found meaning in creating a foundation to help health care workers treat victims of terrorism.[105]

The first June after Chad died I was seeing Mitra, my therapist, weekly. Our main topic of conversation that May was the anxiety leading up to June. Remember June: Chad's birthday, Father's Day, cancer diagnosis, end of school emotions?

---

105 David Kessler, *Finding Meaning: The Sixth Stage of Grief,* 208.

I had brainstormed all sorts of ways to celebrate Chad's birthday and Father's Day—feasts, balloons, outings—when Mitra wondered aloud, "Why don't you plan on volunteering?"

Volunteering? This thought had never crossed my mind. I was so focused on helping myself and my sons survive what I predicted would be a difficult milestone that being selfless and helping others never occurred to me.

The boys and I were going to donate Chad's suits that month to A Wider Circle. This would be the perfect place for us to volunteer. I wanted the boys to see where their dad's suits and dress clothes went and to feel that complete feeling that always fills the heart when I look outside of myself and focus on the greater good.

I signed us up for Father's Day. Matthew and Connor were not particularly keen on doing any sort of work on a weekend, and they weren't much in the mood on that particular holiday. Eventually, though, we all loaded into the car and set off.

An employee greeted us in the lobby and gave us a tour of the facility. Vast warehouse-like rooms were filled with baby clothes, kids' toys, furniture, school supplies, mattresses, and business attire. Matthew and Connor grew interested when we reached this clothing area, scoping out the suits to see if they recognized any of their dad's. The woman guiding us explained how these suits were given to men looking for a job and a home, and how they trained these men with interviewing skills and set them up for success. The boys appeared to appreciate the idea that their father's belongings would continue to bring pride and success to others. Their demeanor changed after that. They now had a spring in their step. They were excited to hear what was next.

We eventually spent the remainder of our time there in the kids' corner. This is the section of the building where parents and children looking to furnish their first apartment were able to choose any toys they wanted. We brought new toys up from the basement and arranged them into appealing arrays for the little ones.

The employees taught us about the concept of "dignity condition," how nothing goes out on the showroom floors that is ripped or stained. This was the first time that any of the three of us had truly thought about the idea of dignity. We took pride in our display of the toys, and we were delighted when a little boy, who looked to be around three-years-old, rushed into the room smiling, laughing, and choosing the loot he would like to take home.

That donation of time and heart turned out to not be selfless at all. It filled our buckets just as much, if not more, than the families who benefited from the items there. Our hearts were full upon leaving, and we continued to volunteer there for years afterward on special occasions.

According to Marianna Pogosyan, PhD, a cultural psychologist, "This 'warm glow' of pro-sociality is thought to be one of the drivers of generous behavior in humans. One reason behind the positive feelings associated with helping others is that being pro-social reinforces our sense of relatedness to others, thus helping us meet our most basic psychological needs." MRIs have recently shown the link between generosity and happiness. Now that I am privy to this secret, I have changed some of our rituals.[106]

For instance, I changed Christmas up a bit that year. At one of Chad's Christmas parties years prior, his boss, John, had shared how part of his children's yearly Christmas budget was allocated to a charity of the child's choice.

As the children got older, they no longer wanted toys, but money. So, John and his wife would allocate a certain amount of money to the gift fund, and a percentage of it would go to charity. That number could be whatever the parents chose: $1, $5, $50; the amount did not matter.

What mattered was the idea of helping the children understand that we give back to those who are less fortunate than ourselves. The first year I adopted this practice, Matthew chose to give to UNICEF because we had just read about an earthquake that had occurred in the Middle East, and he was worried about the children there with no food and water. Connor chose to give to A Wider Circle because that was an organization with which he had experience. In the years following, they chose the Humane Society, Heiffer International, the Multiple Myeloma Research Foundation, and many others. These experiences have helped us all learn empathy and compassion.

Like Peter Alderman's organization that helped to train medical workers to deal with terrorist attacks in memory of his son, some young widows choose to create and participate

---

106 Marianna Pogosyan, "In Helping Others, You Help Yourself."

in organizations relating to the way that their husband died or lived. Whether it be cancer, suicide, heart, military, or hobby-related, rallying around a cause can be fulfilling and invigorating.

When Nicki Bunting's husband, Bubba, died, they had a young son at home, and Nicki was yet to find out that she was pregnant as well. That year, Nicki established a run called Bubba's Belly Run. "That was kind of funny," she laughs. "I called it that because I had a baby in my belly. He was fit and in shape and muscular, but he always had a belly too. The logo was a pregnant woman, but we all knew what the belly really was for."

For three years, Nicki planned and facilitated this run in Bubba's memory. A huge showing of friends and family always came out, and the proceeds went to multiple military organizations. "It kind of gave me purpose for a little while. Even though I had small kids at home, I still needed something to occupy my void time. In fact, it really helped a lot in healing. I didn't know at the time that's what I was doing, but yes that's what I was doing."

Our family has a similar ritual. When he was sick, Chad and I researched multiple organizations focusing on his cancer, multiple myeloma. The MMRF, Multiple Myeloma Research Foundation, seemed most influential in funding research for this type of cancer. Chad was able to attend the race that they held the first year, in 2015 right before he died. We continue to power this engine. Yearly, our friends converge on the National Harbor in support of the cause and our family.

It felt a bit somber the first year, but now it feels more like a celebration. It has turned into a way to remember him officially, gather together, share stories, and show our solidarity and love for him. Our team is often in the top three fundraisers and is always the largest of all the Washington, DC teams.

Being recognized for these awards and seeing all this support boosts my children's spirits and my own each October. It demonstrates how Chad continues to contribute to good, even in death.

This healing by helping others does not just apply to widows and our children. I have to remind myself that it helps others to heal when they help our family. I often feel badly accepting assistance from others, even when they offer. But people want to help. Chad's friends, Scott, Anthony, and Jason, take my boys camping. My dad takes them fishing and to his friend Larry's house to see the cars he has been working on. Chad's friend Oliver has taken them to car shows, basketball games, ziplining, and on multiple other fun excursions.

As great a gift as this is for Connor and Matthew, I know that this is the men's way of connecting with Chad and honoring their friendship even in death.

It may seem counterintuitive because we widows often think of ourselves as the ones in need of help. But helping others truly does plant a seed of humanity in us whose roots reach deep into our hearts and allow hope and happiness to bloom.

CHAPTER 17

RITUALS

For two years now, on her birthday, Mother's Day, and wedding anniversary, Andrea Albanese receives a handwritten note from her husband, Jim. On Valentine's Day, she receives a bouquet of flowers. Jim had the same cancer as Chad, and he died three years ago. During the final months of his life, this thoughtful man spent his time writing cards for all the major events in his children's lives. He even wrote a letter to each of his three daughters to be read on their wedding days. I assume that one day the cards and flowers will cease, but this is a gift that Andrea and their children will cherish forever.

Most of us were not gifted in this way. Our spouses either died suddenly, were too sick to have that sort of attention to detail, or some were just not planners or romantics. So, we are charged to create our own rituals.

"Rituals are actions that symbolically connect us to something meaningful. They can be comforting, express feelings, bring about a sense of closure, or keep an important part of the past alive. When rituals are done to commemorate a loss, they honor both the person who is doing them and the person they've lost," according to David B. Feldman, PhD, a professor in the department of counseling psychology at Santa Clara University and author of multiple books dealing with hope and growth after trauma and loss.

"The symbolism in these rituals can fill us with emotion, give us goosebumps, and punctuate the important events of our lives. Research even shows that some rituals facilitate the body's release of endorphins, which can help reduce anxiety and physical pain."[107]

Sometimes these rituals are grandiose and require loads of effort and planning, like funding a scholarship or managing a nonprofit in a spouse's honor. However, some of the most meaningful rituals are those that only we know about, too seemingly insignificant to even mention. Regardless of their size and reach, these rituals give us the peace and consistency for which we long.

For a long time, I felt like our family didn't have any true traditions and rituals to honor Chad, or the ones we had were not enough. Feldman warns us, though, to "try not to get caught in the trap of thinking that rituals have to be complicated or lengthy. Some are, and some aren't."[108]

Hanging a specific commemorative ornament on the Christmas tree is one of my favorite traditions. It is a heart-shaped glass ornament that says, "In loving memory of Chad

---

107 David Feldman, "The Power of Rituals to Heal Grief."

108 Ibid.

Mortimer O'Neil, 1976-2015." I always place it high in the center of the tree, in front of one of the lights so it sparkles with a halo of yellow around it. These types of rituals are subtle, barely perceptible as traditions, yet they help us do as Feldman says. They take away anxiety and pain and give us peace.

I asked all the widows I interviewed if they had rituals that helped them honor their late spouse. Eighty percent of them started off by saying no. Then, as we spoke, the conversation would steer toward what they do on Father's Day, Mother's Day, birthdays, and anniversaries. Almost all had rituals. They simply didn't consider them hefty enough to be called rituals, or the amount of time that they had spent doing them was not enough to consider them traditions.

The stories of rituals varied. Some families served a favorite meal of the deceased on anniversaries. Some wrote messages on balloons and sent them up into the sky. My sister-in-law's mother, Karla, plans a trip every year on the month of the anniversary of her husband Tony's death. Instead of sitting around depressed, she gets out and lives as Tony would have wanted her to.

In the Jewish religion, it is customary to leave a stone at a person's grave to show that someone has visited. Laura Keller's youngest daughter collects river rocks in places she and her father had travelled together when he lived. She paints and decorates them, and on Father's Day, she visits his grave and delivers these priceless gifts.

Lacey Bruno already had a built-in ritual when her husband Pat died. Pat's mom had passed years earlier, and the Irish family would go visit her at Gates of Heaven Cemetery every St. Patrick's Day. They would buy her green carnations at the cemetery gift shop and bring a pint of Irish whisky, which they proceeded to pour over her grave. When Pat died, he was buried with his mother in the spot that had been slotted for his father. Now, on St. Patrick's Day, Lacey and her son, Ricky, continue this ritual, only they need two bottles of whisky instead of one.

On November 27 each year, the anniversary of Chad's passing, I allow my boys to play hooky from school. Typically, my parents are visiting because it is right around Thanksgiving.

Two years after Chad died, my parents thought we should have a ritual to remember the anniversary of his death. The date was easily swallowed up in Thanksgiving and the busyness of the season. So, they took the boys to the nursery down the road and picked out an evergreen shrub.

Now, every November, the four of them spend time together stringing popcorn and cranberries while sitting around the kitchen table talking and laughing. They bundle up and decorate the tree with the goodies for the birds. Throughout December, we have a gentle reminder of Chad each day as we look out the kitchen window and glimpse the cardinals and wrens eating berries and popcorn off the tree.

Laura Keller finds posting on social media a helpful tradition. "The thing that brings me so much joy are the two times a year I go on Facebook. I post his death day and his birthday."

Each year, Laura recruits her three children to help her write the posts that she will share on those days. She worries that if she writes them, they will be too "maudlin." So, her kids add an element of celebration and happiness. The family looks forward to seeing the likes and the stories that people share in response to their reminder. "It shows he mattered and affected someone, and that people still miss him."

I do the same to help keep Chad's memory alive, and it also helps me not feel so alone. As I scroll down the comments and likes, it is proof to me that he lived. It's like taking a trip down memory lane: his job at the hotels, at corporate, college, our first house, our first neighborhood, childhood families and friends. It often makes me cry to think of all those chapters in life that we had melded together into a beautiful collage. It makes me smile to think that even without him here, this piece of art still exists to remind me. I often wonder for how long I will post on those special dates. There is no right answer, I suppose. I will know when I'm ready to stop.

As much as rituals can help us, sometimes they run their course, which may produce guilt. Charity Yanishak DeNeal talks about how she and her girls had an entire ritual for the anniversary of her husband Drew's death when they lived in Richmond. They would go to Bruster's for a Butterfinger Blizzard because Drew loved the candy bar. Then they would head to the cemetery in downtown Richmond to visit his grave. After that, they ate at Chuy's, Drew's favorite Mexican restaurant.

However, a few years after Drew passed, Charity married Dan. She and her girls moved to Roanoke to live where he worked. Charity says, "It was easier when we lived in the same town where Drew died. I have guilt about not having an easy way to connect to him anymore." With their new surroundings and the girls getting older and harder to pin down, this ritual has naturally faded. The family still sometimes eats Butterfingers or gets Mexican food on his death day, but the urgency and intensity of the custom has changed.

When Nicki Bunting had a two- and a five-year-old at home and Bubba's Belly Walk was just going to be too much for her to organize and manage, she needed to stop doing it. Like Charity, she felt the guilt about cancelling this ritual and was worried that people would judge her for discontinuing it. Not to mention, she was disappointed to no longer see everyone come out in support of Bubba and her family. But she needed to focus on her two little ones at home. She was surprised, in hindsight, of how supportive everyone was of her decision and how no one faulted her for stopping the ritual.

Rituals are meant to help us heal and remember, and so many of them do. According to Mama Donna Henes, contributing author at the *Huffington Post* and ritual expert, "The need for ritual is a basic human instinct, as real, as urgent, and as raw as our need for food, shelter and love. And it is every bit as crucial to our survival." Rituals have been integral in my family's healing. I have found it necessary to reflect and revise some of them, but we keep the ones that make us feel connected to Chad, our friends, our family, and each other—the ones that are crucial to our survival.[109]

---

109 Mama Donna Henes, "Why We Need Rituals in Our Lives."

CHAPTER 18

FOLLOW YOUR HEART

Chad loved music, especially music with strong bass and thundering choruses. "The Wren," an Irish folksong that we listened to at Christmastime, was his favorite. I can still picture him dancing around the house as we hung familiar ornaments on our freshly cut tree. He would lower his voice, tilt his chin downward, and belt out the words in his most baritone voice. He never remembered lyrics, so they would always be wrong, but this made it all the more endearing.

He played the tuba in high school and the beginning of college, a source of pride for his parents and a topic of everlasting amusement for his friends. His parents have pictures in their house of a slight middle school Chad being swallowed up by the huge brass instrument around his neck.

When Chad got sick with cancer and was told that his only hope for recovery would come from a bone marrow transplant, we all were hopeful and started planning. Two of his three brothers were a match. We would need to find a place for him to live near the hospital, schedule friends and family to help take care of him during the dangerous recovery, figure out how to get groceries and meals to him, and collect things to help him pass the time. Chad's father, Deni, had the clever idea of buying him a keyboard. Chad used to enjoy the piano and was actually quite good at it as a child. This would keep him occupied.

When the cancer spread too quickly, and the medicines and trials no longer seemed to have any effect, Chad's body finally gave up fighting and the keyboard sat unused. There was no music left to play, and no one to play it. I put the keyboard in his closet and closed the door.

Little by little, I entered his closet for one reason or another, and the keyboard stood staring at me, a brand-new keyboard sitting in a dead man's closet gathering dust. It struck me as ridiculous. I decided this would not be its fate.

My boys needed to learn to play an instrument, and I had always wanted to sing, so I enlisted all of us in lessons at the local music factory. I gave the boys a choice of instrument; Matthew chose the guitar, Connor the keyboard, and it was voice for me.

The addition of live music has added levity to our world ever since. I look forward to the days now when our instructor Michelle comes to the house to play the piano as I sing or coaches Connor as he plays. In those times, the house fills with the heart-lifting sound of music, the same house that for a year had been much too silent.

Laura Keller's family has used music to heal as well. After Joe died, Laura took the kids to multiple live concerts and musicals. They were an escape from the sorrow that permeated their home. She made sure to share Joe's distinct music taste with her children as she played his CDs during long car trips. At first, they balked at having to listen to his music, but now Johnny Cash and other artists that many teens may never have even heard of top their list of favorites.

Music isn't your thing? Look deep and discover what is. Your thing may be some of the ideas mentioned in previous chapters: creating, volunteering, writing, connecting, religion. All these can be life-affirming. Whatever it is, find what you love and drape yourself in it! Surround yourself with it.

For some women, work is their thing. Kelley Rogers went back to work after her husband John died. She had not worked in twelve years. "Work has been amazing for me. I'm a scientist. I love science. I have a job that's really interesting, and it's like regaining that part of my life, you know, getting validation that I add value to the world. That's been huge because you don't always get that from your kids."

Laura Keller felt the same, especially when her husband was sick. She had just gotten a new job partway through Joe's illness. "I enjoyed being at work. One day I mentioned in passing, 'Oh, my husband is at a chemo treatment because he has pancreatic cancer.'

"My boss was like, '*What?*'"

Laura liked the fact that "it was a place I could be a normal person, not the wife of the person dying of cancer. I sometimes feel badly that I didn't go to every chemo appointment with him. But I wanted to go to work and stop thinking about it; to shut things off."

I often felt the same way about work when Chad was sick and even after he died. It was a place where I felt normal, not focused on sickness, death, and loss. I was allowed only a few days of bereavement leave, which at first, I thought was cruel and unusual. However, returning to a routine and being surrounded by people who cared about me really did help more than hinder. Work now falls into both categories for me at varying times. Sometimes it is a life saver, and other times it is a source of anxiety and stress.

Along the same lines is fitness. Many people would agree that exercise makes them feel amazing when they are finished; however, getting there is what they dread. When I asked Lacey Bruno if she now worries more about her health, she said, "Just the opposite. It became immediately apparent to me after Pat died that I have to be healthy. I have to take care of myself. I'm all my kid has. It is really difficult to find childcare when you need to go and workout, but if you don't make it a priority, you won't do it."

Michelle Steinke-Baumgard, author of the *One Fit Widow* blog and fitness trainer and coach, is the poster child for the importance of exercise in healing from trauma. According to Michelle, there is an:

> *Undeniable connection to our bodies imprint of trauma. This imprint can have severe and lasting effects on our body's critical systems. Chronic pain and even serious illness can be connected to trauma never released within*

our bodies. Our central nervous system, joints, fascia, and muscular systems can store trauma and leave us in debilitating pain.[110]

She goes on to say, "Until body-centered therapy is as widely prescribed as antidepressants and talk therapy, I will keep beating the drum and raising awareness for the importance of a full BODY approach to healing."[111]

Endorphins (chemicals released by our bodies) are produced when we exercise. They help to reduce hormones that cause us stress and anxiety and lead us to an overall feeling of happiness and well-being. Just as Steinke-Baumgard argues, a 1999 study from the "Archives of Internal Medicine" found that exercise can be as effective in treating depression as antidepressant drugs.[112]

Also helpful is the healing force of nature. Kelley Rogers talks about the first five months after they found her husband's body, exercise, nature, and friends are what got her through. "I am so very lucky to have wonderful and wise friends. They took their dogs and I took mine and we hiked. I talked and they listened. I spent a lot of time walking and just feeling nature."

---

110 Michelle Steinke-Baumgard, "Healing from Trauma—Why You Shouldn't Leave Your Body Behind."

111 Ibid.

112 Lakshmy Nair, "How Exercise Improves Mood," *Livestrong*, August 14, 2008.

One of the rituals that my family has made part of our healing is hiking. On dates that would normally bring feelings of sadness and loneliness, we find somewhere new to hike. Thanksgiving, Mother's Day, we hike. Father's Day and Christmas, we hike. I also try to walk the dog every day. Moving my body improves my mood, but nothing feels as good as being outside while doing it.

Activity in green space can be amazingly healing. I took a class this summer about children with ADHD and their brain structures. I was fascinated by recent studies that revealed how playing outside in green space helps children with ADHD focus and maintain emotional balance in a way that playing on blacktop and in gyms cannot. It is not just the exercise that helps them but nature itself.

In a study out of Harvard Medical School in 2018 focusing on aging men, Dr. Jason Strauss, director of geriatric psychiatry at Harvard-affiliated Cambridge Health Alliance, said that because older men may suffer from depression and anxiety due to life changes that come with age, they may want to forego medicine and opt for interactions with nature. Even twenty to thirty minutes in nature three days a week is sufficient in boosting mood, according to Strauss. Just listening to nature sounds or looking at pictures of nature can also be beneficial.[113]

Equally as interesting: crying can improve mood. As I mentioned in the chapter about fears, I often have heart palpitations. I have linked the cause of these to stress, and I have

113 "Sour Mood Getting You Down?"

found that when I allow myself to slow down enough to feel the sadness, the palpitations ease. Andrea Albanese refers to this as the "grief zit."

I know, I know. The mental image this evokes is repulsive, but the analogy is spot on. The pressure that builds as we move forward with our lives, trying not to feel too much, not to cry, not to give into our sadness, eventually needs to be released.

My place of release used to be in Chad's office, where I would shut myself in to cry at night after Matthew and Connor went to sleep. I made a playlist of all the saddest songs about loss (I have added some of these titles, as well as some songs to bring you strength, at the end of the book). I would cycle through artist after artist lamenting the losses of girlfriends, boyfriends, love, everything one could lose in this ephemeral world. I would watch the video that I made for Chad's funeral. This weeping ritual helped to calm and center me. I would wake up the next day feeling peaceful.

Melanie Green plans times to cry as well. "I had my days off work. Those were my scheduled days where I could cry. I just liked to freely express my grief if I wanted to. Quarantine messed up my process though because now my kids are home all the time." Melanie would play music, look through Jon's belongings, read old cards, or drive in her car alone to put herself in that space.

Many of the widows with whom I spoke had some sort of ritual for allowing themselves to pop that grief zit. For many, it was driving in the car alone. Heather Hofmann says, "I think of him when I'm driving. That's the only time it ever hits me. It is there instantly. Right away I am crying, in shock or completely depressed, completely alone."

This may sound sad to some, but crying is cathartic. I always feel better after a really good uncontrolled cry. The Japanese agree. They have something called "crying clubs" where people come together just to cry. They believe that this releases stress and keeps them mentally sound.[114]

Studies have proven this to be true. According to Stephen Sideroff, PhD, a clinical psychologist at UCLA and director of the Raoul Wallenberg Institute of Ethics, tears that stem from emotions (rather than just wind or sand in your eyes) actually contain higher levels of stress hormones than other tears, and they contain higher levels of manganese that helps to regulate mood. He says that crying "activates the parasympathetic nervous system and restores the body to a state of balance." No wonder crying makes us feel better.[115]

Kelley Rogers, my neighborhood friend who lost her husband John, shared with me a philosophy she calls Big Me and Little Me:

> *There's a Little Me and a Big Me. The Big Me is so grateful for all the blessings and support that I have. Because of the Big Me, I can keep my head up and my eyes on what's really important. This is how we get through. But then there's Little Me. Little Me is so mad. My life is taking care of everybody else's needs, never having any time for*

---

114 Serusha Govender, "Is Crying Good for You?"

115 Ibid.

myself, and having all this work dumped on me. So, I have to give myself time to be Little Me. Then I have more space to be Big Me.

Just knowing that both Little Me and Big Me exist in all of us is comforting. Sometimes we want to curl into a ball and scream at the top of our lungs how unfair all of this is. With this we feed the Little Me. Sometimes we are able to focus on joy and fulfillment, and we feed the Big Me. Both must be nurtured. Without feeding the Little, we can't grow the Big.

Making conscious choices to do what we need helps us heal, making space for the things that fill your heart, making time for them, moving aside plans to fit them in. As we all know full well, we only get one chance at this. We have only one life. We owe it to ourselves to live it well. If not for ourselves, we owe it to those who were not given the opportunity.

CHAPTER 19

DATING

"I can't believe you are still single."
"It's been over a year now."
"You'll move on."
"You are young. You will find someone else."

These are the types of hurtful iterations, often couched within kinder contexts, that young widows hear from the most well-meaning friends, family, and strangers as time moves forward after loss. These comments make me feel as if I should be healing faster as if the years of life that I spent with Chad were just plots on a line graph getting me from there to here. Sterile. Emotionless. They imply that, now that some time has passed, I should be fine.

When a story is told of a young widow, the question immediately following is, "How long ago did her husband die?" I'm guilty of this myself. It's as if we, as a society, draw an imaginary line in the sand deeming an appropriate amount of time for grieving. Then, when the widow has crossed that line, she should be up and out, looking to remarry again.

This not only assumes there is a specific time when we can say we are recovered enough to look for new love, but it also assumes that finding another partner will solve all our problems. I assert that neither is true. Every woman grieves in her own way, on her own timeline. And, judging from the more than 39 percent of marriages that end in divorce, a life partner clearly does not guarantee a happily ever after.[116]

In C.S. Lewis's book, *A Grief Observed*, Carol negates the idea that we ever completely get over our loss when he draws the parallel between loss of a spouse and loss of a leg. "He will probably have recurrent pains in the stump all his life. And perhaps pretty bad ones. And he will always be a one-legged man." He continues, "At present, I am learning to get about on crutches. Perhaps I shall presently be given a wooden leg, but I shall never be a biped again."[117]

The loss we endure and the relationship we had with our spouse will forever exist as part of us. We would not be who we are without both. However, David Kessler has found that "your heart can have many loves in its lifetime. A new love can grow out of the same soil without diminishing a past love."[118]

In her *One Fit Widow* blog, Michelle Steinke-Baumgard, who remarried after the loss of her husband Mitch, recognizes that love does not have to be "mutually exclusive." She asserts

---

116 Belinda Luscombe, "The Divorce Rate is Dropping: That May Not Actually Be Good News."

117 C.S. Lewis, *A Grief Observed*..

118 David Kessler, *Finding Meaning: The Sixth Stage of Grief*, 94.

that "great love enhances your capacity for more great love in your life. Love expands the heart, even if a hole remains."[119]

With this hope, some young widows are willing to enter into the brave new world of dating. I entered the dating world about a year after Chad passed away. I had never doubted that I would want to date again one day. I remember telling my friend, Daphne, just a month after Chad passed that I could potentially be with the next person for longer than I was with Chad.

I was thirty-nine years old. Chad was my very best friend. I missed his companionship. I missed having a male adult to go to dinner with, to travel with, just to talk with about grown-up topics. I missed having someone to call when I was having an amazing day or a crappy one.

Lacey Bruno, who lost her husband fifteen years ago, articulates the ache of missing a spouse:

> *I've been alive for fifty-three years, and I have only been married five of those years. There is something you miss about that commitment you make to a husband. It's not the same as just dating someone, and there is nobody on this earth who knew me like that man.*

Some young widows choose to not date at all. When I mention my dating life to my friend Heather Hofmann, who lost her husband two years ago, she says, "That makes me want to throw up. I can't even imagine doing that right now."

---

119 Michelle Steinke-Baumgard, "I May Be Remarried, But I'm Still a Widow."

Some are on the fence. Melanie Green lost her husband, Jon, two years ago. Jon was her high school sweetheart. When I asked her if she would ever consider dating, she said, "I want to and I should, but I'm just having a hard time wrapping my heart around that. I think that's where my guilt would come in. But do I want to be in this state the rest of my life? Hell no!"

Some widows realize they would like the companionship once their children are almost grown and out of the house. Laura Keller, who lost her husband five years ago, says, "I have not even wanted to date until recently. But all of the kids will be in college soon. What is my life going to look like?" A few years prior, her three children wanted nothing to do with their mom dating or remarrying. Recently, though, they turned a corner and told Laura they wanted to make her a dating profile. Laura is still skeptical. "It's just too much to deal with," she sighs.

Lacey Bruno recently started dating again now that her son is in high school. She says, "I get scared of countless hours that I have to fill alone. Every decade of your life, you are a different you. And I'm okay with that. I like the person I am now better than the person I was back then. But I will never have that relationship again. It's never going to be the same."

It is never going to be the same again as it was with your spouse, but different is not always bad.

After twenty-some years as a couple, my standards are not set anymore. In the beginning of my dating journey, I had to redefine what exactly I was looking for in this "Chapter Two" of my life. I was not necessarily looking for Chad again. There were characteristics of Chad that would be non-negotiables for me in finding my next match: loyalty, honesty, strong work ethic, humor, adventurousness, passion.

On the other hand, some of my top priorities when I was twenty-four were no longer important to me. For instance, I was no longer looking for someone to have children with or to support us as we went through the struggles of the childrearing years. I had changed in the twenty years since we started dating, and so had my needs and desires.

My therapist suggested I make a list of everything important to me in the man that I was searching for. She told me to put this list out to the universe (sounds far out, but I liked the idea) and to see what came to me. She told me to carry the list with me at all times and refer back to it periodically. I call this my "Universe List," and I still keep it in the notes section on my phone. Here's the list that continues to evolve:

Universe List

- Kind
- Funny—makes me laugh
- Handsome (to me at least!)
- Likable
- Similar interests
- Positive
- Smart
- Adventurous
- Understanding
- Likes a woman with her own mind
- Loves me unconditionally

- Makes me feel good about myself
- Supports my decisions
- Present
- Hard working
- Flexible
- Likes to travel
- Learner
- Good communicator
- Financially independent
- Family guy
- Loves his kids (if has them)
- Enjoys my kids, and vice versa
- We don't have to move schools
- Had a good or decent marriage
- Kind about ex-wife
- Has friends (whom I like)
- Healthy
- No drugs or smoking
- No major mental health issues
- Comes from a good family

Widows are in a unique spot when it comes to dating. Most men in the dating world are not widowers. Instead, they are divorced or have never been married. It is difficult trying to explain my husband to a date. I sound like an eighty-year-old woman if I say my "late husband." I feel like I am putting off the aura of clinging to the past when I say, "my husband." Typically, I try to use Chad's name as early in the conversation as possible so that I can just say "Chad" when referring to him. People who are divorced easily say, "my ex."

Some women choose not to talk about their late husbands at all because they do not want their dates to think they are hung up on them. This approach doesn't work for me. Many widows were married for years before their spouse died. I have actually had to tell a man whom I was dating that if he didn't ask about Chad, he would lose twenty plus years of my history—of who *I* am. Not to mention, if we had ended up together, how would that be for my children to feel as if the subject of their father were taboo? I had to break up with him because he never felt comfortable with the subject.

To me, the ideal partner would be a man who understands that a woman can love a person who is no longer on this earth while still loving the person in front of her.

Kerry Phillips, author of the *Young, Widowed, and Dating: Restarting Your Heart After Death Do Us Part* blog clarifies that "as amazing as my new guy is, he was never designed to fit into that spot. That spot will always belong to the man who came before him. But he has carved out his own place in my heart—coordinates that belong to him and him alone."[120]

Charity Yanishak DeNeal, whose husband Drew passed away after six years with brain cancer, remarried a few years ago. She spoke of how difficult it was when she first started dating Dan. He was divorced, and he was used to dating people who had negative feelings about their past relationships. He never had dated a widow before.

---

120 Kerry Phillips, "But You're with Someone New—Why the Grief?"

Charity and Drew's families would often share stories about Drew with Dan around. Her girls would, of course, talk about their father. Dan was great about this, but at times it made him uncomfortable.

After a while, he and Charity worked out a pact that when he felt uncomfortable about something, he would talk to her about it. It has gotten easier for both as time has moved on. He is often now the one who prompts Charity to celebrate Drew's birthday and the anniversary of his death. It takes a strong man to accept that a widow will never stop loving her husband and a confident man to understand that she has room in her heart for both.

I could write an entire book on my dating adventures over the past four years, but suffice it to say, I have enjoyed most of them. I have a rule that I leave my children no more than once a week with a babysitter. So, due to my lack of opportunity to meet single men, most of my experiences have come from online dating. I have met a couple of men through friends as well. I could have been good friends with most of the men I have met. I enjoyed their company, but I couldn't imagine myself with them romantically.

The problem with this, of course, is that most forty-something men are not looking to add to their friend collection. I struggle with this because I often don't know if I should waste my time or theirs going out on a third or fourth date. I like them, but as an eighth-grade girl might say, "Do I *like, like* him?"

What has helped me with this issue was a post in Mark Manson's blog, *Life Advice That Doesn't Suck*. The post is called "Fuck Yes or No"—inappropriate name, completely appropriate way to explain the theory. The premise is that unless you are both thinking *Fuck yes*! about seeing each other again, being physical, introducing each other to friends, then the clear answer is "no." That person is not right for you. Manson says, "If you are in the gray area to begin with, you've already lost." I have found this to be true time and time again, and this advice has been a clear guide for me in this new terrain.[121]

The hardest part about dating as a widow is allowing yourself to feel vulnerable. Brené Brown says, "Embracing our vulnerabilities is risky but not nearly as dangerous as giving up on love and belonging and joy—the experiences that make us the most vulnerable." Widows have lost a lot. The last thing they want is to lose again. Rejection and loss are close cousins, and they are what I fear most about allowing someone new into my heart.[122]

I don't allow my children to meet anyone for at least a few months or until I feel like the relationship is strong enough to stick. I have made the mistake of introducing my children to a man whom I thought would be around for a while, and then he ended the relationship without warning. My children were devastated. I was devastated. It took me months of introspection to realize that he never was the right person for me.

---

121 Mark Manson, "Fuck Yes or No," *Mark Manson: Life Advice That Doesn't Suck*.

122 Brené Brown, *The Gifts of Imperfection*, 6.

As Jay Shetty, a motivational speaker and blogger whose teachings are rooted in his years as a monk, says, "In our pain we find our greatest power."[123] He reminds us that "it's in those moments that feel like the death of our dreams, that our truest potential is actually taking birth. If a door doesn't open, it's not your door."[124] I learned so much from feeling the pain of dating rejection. As much as it hurt, it led me to life-altering realizations. It led me to finally write this book. I decided to travel with my girlfriends, mom, and sister-in-law. I went back to appreciating and spending more time with my kids. Thank God that that door was not mine.

My friend Andrea began dating her boyfriend, Dave, a year after her husband passed. Andrea and Dave had a ton in common. He had six children. She had five. They were devout Catholics. They found in each other a sounding board because they had both lost their spouses. However, after two years of a strong relationship, it ended.

Andrea found herself heartbroken. She felt like she had regressed back to the day Jim had died. Dave was her reprieve from the day in and out with her children, from the judgmental eyes all around her. The other day she texted me wondering, "Is the only way to heal by dating someone else?" She has asked me this a number of times. I'm no expert, but I honestly think the answer is no.

I purposefully positioned this chapter at the end of the book because, at least in my case, I had a lot of healing and soul

---

123 Jay Shetty, "If You've Been Rejected—Watch This," 3:14.

124 Shetty, "Rejected," 2:48.

searching to do before I could be ready to invite anyone else into my life again.

To borrow a line from Mr. Rogers, "You can't really love someone else unless you really love yourself."

I found dating to be addictive. I love getting dressed up, putting on makeup and heels, and feeling attractive. It is a far cry from my daily life of black yoga pants and baggy sweatshirts. I like conversation with men, the attention of men, intimacy with men, and quite honestly, the break from the stresses of life.

When I am involved with someone, I eat less, feel happier, and I am generally a more confident, less anxious person. That is all lovely, as long as I am mindful of what is making me feel this way.

When the excitement ends and the relationship fizzles, I end up feeling like I am back where I started when Chad died. I have in time come to realize that I'm not. It's just that after feeling those high highs, not much can compare. If I am not cognizant of what is happening, though, I can spiral down that black hole of self-doubt and self-pity. That is not the place for me.

I, of course, still picture being swept off my feet by a handsome man who happens to love kids, adores me, and I adore him back. We would have a lovely fall wedding in a barn at a winery with a breathtaking view.

Until this knight in shining armor arrives, I am not willing to settle. The first thing that Matthew and Connor both asked when I told them Chad was sick and again when I told them he died was, "Will you get married again?" I have heard this same story from a number of widows and widowers. Children feel a hole that needs to be filled. Fill it with someone else, and all will be fine. Sometimes adults feel this way too. I have decided to hold out for someone who feels just right.

I'm willing to ride this roller coaster for at least a while longer. I had one great love. I hope to have another. Even if that never happens, I will continue to consider myself incredibly fortunate. Plus, I kind of like who I am becoming on the ride.

SECTION 5.

A NEW HORIZON

"You know, happiness can be found even in the darkest of times, if one only remembers to turn on the light."

~ALBUS DUMBLEDORE, *HARRY POTTER AND THE PRISONER OF AZKABAN*

CHAPTER 20

FINDING HOPE

I have always seen artists depict the lotus flower as a symbol of beauty, but I didn't realize the backstory of this unique flower until recently. After some research, I found that the most beautiful lotus flowers emerge from muddy, murky waters.

The flower maintains its beauty every day when it reblooms because its petals are covered in a layer of wax that does not let it wither or crush under the weight of the heavy mud. According to Katie Robinson, writer for *Town & Country Magazine*, "It continues to resurrect itself, coming back just as beautiful as it was last seen. With such refusal to accept defeat."[125]

So it goes for the young widow. Despite subpar conditions, rooted in the muck of loss, we reemerge bolder, wiser, and kinder from our struggle. Being a young widow is physically and emotionally draining, yet we discover ways to make

125 Katie Robinson, "The Secret Meaning of the Lotus Flower."

meaning and find beauty in life. Elisabeth Kübler-Ross recognizes that:

> *The most beautiful people we have known are those who have known defeat, known suffering, known struggle, known loss, and have found their way out of the depths. These persons have an appreciation, a sensitivity, and an understanding of life that fills them with compassion, gentleness, and a deep loving concern. Beautiful people do not just happen.*[126]

Digging out from the depths and emerging stronger does not just happen, nor is it easy.

In those early days after Chad died, I was surrounded by sadness. Friends who brought casseroles were sorrowful. Coworkers wore looks of pity as they approached me. My family and Chad's were suddenly different, our edges worn. Tears were greetings. I was convinced that this mood would surround the remainder of my life—dark, morose, somber.

However, little by little, the light reemerged. As C.S. Lewis describes his healing after H, his wife, passed from cancer, "There was no sudden striking and emotional transition, like the warming of a room or the coming of daylight. When you first notice them, they have already been going on for some time."[127]

---

126 Elisabeth Kübler Ross, *Death: The Final Stage of Growth*, 96.

127 C.S. Lewis. *A Grief Observed.*

Similarly, one day I realized that the grief load had been lightening for a while. It hit me that I had been smiling and laughing more often; that I had again started to live. That is not to say, five years after loss, I don't tear up when I drive away from dropping Connor at camp and glimpse him in the rearview mirror, still waving goodbye after his friends have all gone, for fear that he will never see me again, or when I am talking to Matthew about his dad, and he pretends his eyes itch as he tries to wipe away the tears.

But that paralyzing pain has let up, and I have begun to experience joy again.

Kessler recognizes that "none of us know how long we have. Five minutes, five years, or fifty years. We don't have that kind of control. But we do have control over how we choose to spend whatever time remains to us."[128]

In the previous chapters, I described patterns that I have witnessed in widows whom I admire, my beacons of hope, the ones who are truly life-filled. The widows who have taken lemons and made the best doggone spiked lemonade anyone has ever tasted. Again, these women still hurt. They still grieve. They still struggle.

Through their struggle, though, they have become what Brené Brown would call a wild heart. "The mark of a wild heart is living out the paradox of love in our lives. It's the ability to be tough and tender, excited and scared, brave and afraid—all in the same moment. It's showing up in our vulnerability and

128 David Kessler, *Finding Meaning: The Sixth Stage of Grief*, 6.

our courage, being both fierce and kind."[129] They never chose to be a part of this club, but they have bravely and fiercely decked out the clubhouse.

After losing a spouse, life forces us to forge new identities. This takes focus and time spent on what makes us joyful and fills us with hope. It takes conscious decision making about what does not fulfill us and needs to be purged. There is no straight line that takes us to a physical finish line. There is no true final destination. The joy is found in the journey, and many times in the little things that we would have formerly overlooked.

This young widow's journey often reminds me of a children's book by Michael Rosen, *We're Going on a Bear Hunt.* My children loved on this board book so much when they were young our copy was covered in rips, tears, and baby teeth marks. I could recite it in my sleep.

In the story, the family is presented with all sorts of obstacles while trying to hunt down a bear. Each time something comes in the way of them reaching their goal, they momentarily hesitate. Then they decide,

> *We can't go over it.*
> *We can't go under it.*
> *Oh no!*
> *We have to go through it.*[130]

---

129 Brené Brown, *Braving the Wilderness*, 155.

130 Michael Rosen, *Going on a Bear Hunt*, 2.

This tale of perseverance is so much like the tale of the young widow's voyage forward. As much as we may want to cut corners and "get over" our grief, it is a process we all have to go through. The only way forward is through. For some, "through" is more difficult than for others. Complicated grief, multiple losses, mental illness, financial struggles, and other situations that exacerbate grief and trauma often coexist.

We alone chart the way through now. We are at the helm. We may choose to allow negativity and doubt to take up space in our minds and our lives. We may choose to allow people in who don't help us grow or move forward. We may let the guilt of things that happened in the past devour us. Or we may infuse our lives with jobs that fulfill us, connections that expand us, hobbies that excite us, and rituals that keep our loved ones present. The choice is ours.

The light is ours to switch on. Amidst the waves of emotions, happiness is there to be found, even when it feels like only darkness remains. We must discover what brings us light—no one is able to do this for us—and surround ourselves with those things. We must allow ourselves to feel the darkness and to grieve, but we cannot get stuck there.

There is life to be lived, destinations unexplored, and magic still to happen on this detoured journey.

Bon voyage, my beautiful widow sister. I wish you a bright passage forward.

ACKNOWLEDGMENTS

I would first like to thank my sons, Connor and Matthew. You are my heart. Writing this book was not easy, and there were days when I wanted to give up, but knowing you were watching always led me to persevere. You are both amazing and resilient. Every day, I learn from you the importance of laughter, silliness, and joy. I love you more than words can ever express.

With love to my mom and dad, the first people who ever believed in my ability to write and to make a difference—the people who instilled in me a curiosity and love of learning and books. You have been my greatest source of strength throughout my life. I learned from you that life isn't always easy and that we all get knocked down and hurt. But it is all worth standing back up for. Thank you for always being there to offer your hands.

Thank you from the bottom of my heart to the young widows who were so brave to share their stories throughout the pages of this book. I am inspired by you all. Love and thanks to:

Andrea Albanese
Charity Yanishak DeNeal
Melanie Green
Laura Keller
Heather Hofmann
Lacey Bruno
Laura Keller
Kelley Rogers
Nicki Bunting
Andrea Phipps
Teresa Snow

Thank you also to my best friend Heather Bianchi, who read the heck out of my drafts and gave me important perspective and feedback that truly improved my writing; and to Allison Soled, who was there with me every step of the way in this labor of love as we both wrote our books together.

Huge thanks from the bottom of my heart to all of my family and friends who purchased *At the Helm* during its presale campaign. Without you, this book would not exist. I took a leap of faith, and you all were there to catch me. Thank you for your support and your belief in me:

Masoud Edalatkhah, Oliver Meinzer, Marsha and George Fraunfelder, Lisa Merkel, Lisa Narges, Theresa Frazier, Sarah Heitzler, Erin Smeller, Stephanie Kauffman, Ashley LeFave, Nancy Fraunfelder, Aileen Gregory, Lauren Collogan, Katy and Rob Engels, Tina Miller, Corey Garver, Aubrey Ciatto, Abbey Lewis, Michelle McKee, Debbie Buteau, Kristin Francis, Jill Rifkin, Rebecca Kotok, Gretchen Hays, Anita Khatiwara, Amy Gorman, Melissa Mostrom, Robin

Giordano, Anne Eubank, Katie Hecklinger, Kimberly Sweeney, Tracy Wills Zapata, Linda Labarge, Kristen Howard, Marie Browne, Anthony Martineau, Patricia Litwin, Scott Mitchell, Eric Koester, John Whitwell, Beth Johnson, Dena Johnson, Anthony Perone, Mindy Van Valkenburgh, Nicole Ball, Scott Hansen, James O'Neil, Sue Gottlieb, Elizabeth Luecking, Katie Walsh Caffrey, Christine O'Donnell, Brittany Do, Lisa Cline, Robert and Judie Sickley, Theresa Ling-While, Karen Traub, Lindsey Hoggle, Jodi Johnson, Kelly McAleer, Debra Kostyo, Jennifer McLennan, Wendy Owens, Mary Roberts, Sharon Cassidy, Nura Mendez, Anne Marie Mumper, Helen Guyton, Sandy Pearce, Benjamin Wilhelm, Jason Pressly, Denise Naguib, Charity Yanishak DeNeal, Dana Varadiova, Katherine Gruell, Vicki Mostrom, Laura Moody, Melissa O'Neil, Nicki Bunting, Erika Huyck, Dehna Richards, Peggy Laver, Martha Timmons, Laurie Oyer, Ursula Petricek, Anna Maria Kittleson, Genevieve LaClair, Shay Thompson, Katherine Bohn, Sue Peterson, Kristina Stracke, Jessica Shevitz, Jason Paugys, Jennifer LaHart, Karen Taylor, Deb Ousey, Monica McGee, Stephanie Brant, Melanie Green, Meredith Shankle, Jennifer Whitman, Doug Clarke, Jenna Blinn, April O'Neil, Mitzi Harlor, Joelly Belman, Thalia Tobin, Kelly McAleer, Susan Kohler, Bridgid McKelvey, David Salpeter, Eudora Miller, Allyson Buck, Richard O'Neil, Jennifer Legge, Allison Soled, Michelle Wilson, Lynn Embs, Heather Rose, Dove Payman, Laura Greene, Dave Rondeau, Valerie Vinson, Jodi Grubb, Jamie Miller, Meredith Bollini, Jill Straniero, Katherine Sheridan Macomber, Laura Pierce, Deborah Waechter, Sharon Becker, Tara DeCapite, Kelley Rogers, Jane Gromelski, Andrea Albanese, Kim Dalin, Karen Barnett, David Becker, Emma Hagen, Malena Boyle, Christy Jenkins, Molly Lichtenstein, Margie

Elberson, Amy Modini, Kathryn DiParisi, Lacey Bruno, Kim Kaneshige, Chris Adams, Randi Mack, Daniela Jacobs, Sarah Held, Jolene Baxter, Amy Garver, Erin Smith, Salm Spina, Amy Jordan, Heather Santoro, JoAnn Catalano, Lora Harmon, Lori Sweeney, Chintimini Keith, Terri and Deni O'Neil, Jamie Stratford, Shannon Fraunfelder, Heather Bianchi, Heather Hofmann, Ryan O'Neil, Katja Zuras, Julie Vanas, Joan Mody, Karen Zappone, Megan Marzluff, Katie Krolczyk, Miguel Falcon, Tara Bissett, Robert Scheer, Lydia Kline, and Megan Nuell.

Thanks to the Facebook Young Widows and Widowers Support Group who helped me compile a list of the saddest and strongest songs a young widow could wish for.

Thank you also to the team who walked me through writing this book baby step by baby step. Thank you to Eric Koester of Creator Institute and Georgetown University for teaching me the ins and outs of manuscript creation. Thank you to my developmental editor, Anne Kelley, for setting me on the right track, and to Julie Colvin, my marketing and revisions editor and fellow widow, for polishing what was rough and sharing her personal as well as professional feedback. Our pairing was a gift.

And last, but certainly not least, thank you to all my friends and coworkers who made the lonely task of authoring a book during a pandemic more tolerable. I would have lost my mind without you all!

SONGS TO CRY TO

"Dancing with Your Ghost," Sasha Sloan
"When a Heart Breaks," Ben Rector
"Photograph," Ed Sheeran
"It's so Hard to Say Goodbye," Boys II Men
"Temporary Home," Carrie Underwood
"See You Again," Carrie Underwood
"Drink a Beer," Luke Bryan
"Like I'm Gonna Lose You," Meghan Trainor
"Mine Would Be You," Blake Shelton
"Memories," Maroon 5
"Five More Minutes," Scotty McCreery
"Always Remember Us This Way," Lady Gaga
"I'll Never Love Again," Lady Gaga
"One Sweet Day," Boyz II Men and Mariah Carey
"Dancing in the Sky," Dani and Lizzy
"Jealous of the Angels," Donna Taggart
"Over You," Miranda Lambert
"Drowning," Chris Young (watch the video—tears)
"Show Me Around," Carly Pearce
"You Said You'd Grow Old with Me," Michael Schulte

"Probably Wouldn't Be This Way," Leann Rimes
"Used to You," Luke Combs
"Look You Up," Caleche Ryder
"Beam Me Up," Pink
"Nobody But You," Blake Shelton and Gwen Stefani
"Love Lives On," Mallary Hope
"Lay Me Down," Sam Smith
"Hold On," Chord Overstreet
"You Should Be Here," Cole Swindell
"The Flame," Cheap Trick
"Someone You Loved," Lewis Capaldi
"See You Again," Charlie Puth and Wiz Khalifa
"There You'll Be," Faith Hill
"Because You Loved Me," Celine Dion
"Miss You All Time," O.A.R.
"We Were," Keith Urban
"If You're Reading This," Tim McGraw (armed forces specific)
"Before You Go," Lewis Capaldi (suicide specific)
"Play This When I'm Gone," Machine Gun Kelly (suicide specific)

SONGS TO GIVE YOU STRENGTH

"Fly," Maddie & Tae
"One Less Day (Dying Young)," Rob Thomas
"Wait for It," Leslie Odom Jr.
"This Is Me," Keala Settle
"You Say," Lauren Daigle
"Rescue," Lauren Daigle
"The Dance," Garth Brooks
"Home," Chris Tomlin
"I Was Born," Hanson
"GET UP," Shinedown
"When We Fall Apart," Ryan Stevenson
"The Greatest," Sia
"Tell Your Heart to Beat Again," Danny Gokey
"And It's Still Alright," Nathaniel Rateliff
"When I Get Where I'm Going," Brad Paisley and Dolly Parton
"In My Life," The Beatles
"In My Blood," Shawn Mendes

"Fight Song," Rachel Platten
"Be a Light," Thomas Rhett
"Be Still," The Fray
"Starting Over," Chris Stapleton
"How They Remember You," Rascal Flatts

ADDITIONAL RESOURCES

CAMPS FOR GRIEVING CHILDREN

- Camp Erin is free to children (ages 6–17) grieving the death of a significant person in their lives: elunanetwork.org/camps-programs/camp-erin/

- Camp Kesem is free to children (ages 6–18) with a parent who has or has died from cancer: www.campkesem.org

- Experience Camp is free to children and teens who have experienced the death of a parent, sibling or primary caregiver: www.experiencecamps.org

- Comfort Zone Camp is free to children and young adults (ages 7–25) parents, sibling, or legal guardian: comfortzonecamp.org

- Outward Bound for Grieving Teens consists of seven-day excursions for grieving teens (ages 14–17). Camp costs are significantly reduced by donors: https://www.outward-bound.org/group-programs/grieving-teens/

NATIONAL ORGANIZATIONS TO SUPPORT GRIEVING FAMILIES

- The National Alliance for Grieving Children—this site houses a wealth of knowledge of how to help parents and children of all ages manage grief. You can also search by state to find what opportunities are available near you: https://childrengrieve.org/

- The Hospice Foundation of America's site gives resources for helping children deal with death. Your local hospice will likely be able to give you more information about programs and supports in your area: https://hospicefoundation.org/Grief-(1)/Children-and-Grief

- The Dinner Party, a national organization that hosts get-togethers aimed at young adults who have lost a parent: https://www.thedinnerparty.org/

- HealGrief links teens and young adults to a digital community of others with similar losses: https://healgrief.org/amf-app/

- The Widowed Parent Podcast—experts and non-experts covers all sorts of topics about being a widowed parent: https://jennylisk.com/

FINANCIAL SUPPORT FOR YOUNG WIDOWS

Government Resources:

- Social Security Administration: www.ssa.gov/benefits/survivors/ifyou.html
- Veterans Administration: https://www.va.gov/pension/survivors-pension/
- Various Other Benefits: benefits.gov

Grassroots Foundations:

- Ted Lindeman Outreach Foundation: tedlindemanoutreachfoundation.com
- Acts of Simple Kindness: karen@actsofsimplekindness.org
- The Liz Logelin Foundation: thelizlogelinfoundation.org
- Hope for Widows Foundation: hopeforwidows.org

APPENDIX

CHAPTER 1

Encyclopedia.com, s.v. "Widows and Widowers." Accessed December 20, 2020, https://www.encyclopedia.com/international/encyclopedias-almanacs-transcripts-and-maps/widows-and-widowers#:~:text=Through%20most%20of%20European%20history%2C%20the%20death%20of,emotional%20and%20economic%20support%20for%20the%20surviving%20partner.

Henderson, Beau. "Five Surprising Facts About Widowhood." *The Good Men Project*, June 21, 2020. https://goodmenproject.com/featured-content/five-surprising-facts-about-widowhood/.

Isaacs, Florence. "Why More Widowers Date, Remarry Than Widows." *Legacy Connect* (blog). March 18, 2015. http://connect.legacy.com/profiles/blogs/why-more-widowers-date-remarry-than-widows.

Modern Widows Club. "Origen of the Word Widow." Accessed December 20, 2020. https://modernwidowsclub.com/origin-of-the-word-widow/.

United Nations. "Invisible Women, Invisible Problems." Accessed December 20, 2020. https://www.un.org/en/observances/widows-day.

Zavada, Jack. "Introduction to the Book of Ruth." *Learn Religions*, January 4, 2020. https://www.learnreligions.com/book-of-ruth-701118.

CHAPTER 2

Bonanno, George. *The Other Side of Sadness*. Read by Jonathan Todd Ross. Basic Books, 2019. Audible audio ed., 9 hours, 9 minutes.

Doughty, Elizabeth A., Adriana Wissel, and Cynthia Glorfield. *Current Trends in Grief Counseling.* Paper based on a program presented at the 2011 American Counseling Association and Exposition, March 23-27, 2011. Alexandria: Vistas Online, 2011. Accessed December 20, 2020. https://www.counseling.org/resources/library/vistas/2011-V-Online/Article_94.pdf.

Kübler-Ross, Elisabeth, and David Kessler. *On Grief and Grieving: Finding the Meaning of Grief Through the Five Stages of Loss.* New York: Scribner, 2005.

Neimeyer, Robert. "The Dual Process Model." De School voor Transitie. Streamed live on September 14 and 15. YouTube video, 2:23-5:59. https://www.bing.com/videos/searchq=dual+process+model+of+grief&docid=608044039180780602&mid=12F75E0D6DD4F4C750A512F75E0D6DD4F4C750A5&view=detail&FORM=VIRE.

Psychology Today. "Post-Traumatic Growth." Accessed December 20, 2020. https://www.psychologytoday.com/us/basics/post-traumatic-growth.

Sandberg, Sheryl, and Adam Grant. *Option B: Facing Adversity, Building Resilience, and Finding Joy.* New York: Alfred A. Knopf, 2017.

Steinke-Baumgard, Michelle. *Healthy Healing: A Guide to Working Out Grief.* New York: Harper-Collins, 2017.

Warburton, Geoff. "The Adventures of Grief." Filmed November 15, 2012 in Brighton, United Kingdom, TED video, 11:59. https://www.youtube.com/watch?v=juET61B1P98&feature=emb_logo.

CHAPTER 3

Cake. "Nine Things to do with Your Wedding Ring After a Spouse's Death." Accessed December 20, 2020. https://www.joincake.com/blog/what-to-do-with-wedding-ring-after-death/.

Kessler, David. *Finding Meaning: The Sixth Stage of Grief.* New York: Scribner, 2019.

CHAPTER 4

Feintuch, Stacy. "Facebook Can Be Hard." *Widow Wears Pink* (blog). *Living the Second Act*, September 15, 2016. https://livingthesecondact.com/2016/09/15/facebook/.

Hollis, Rachel. *Girl, Stop Apologizing: A Shame-Free Plan for Embracing and Achieving Your Goals.* USA: Harper Collins Leadership, 2019.

Kessler, David. *Finding Meaning: The Sixth Stage of Grief.* New York: Scribner, 2019.

Lynn, Kelly. "When Someone You Love Dies, There Is No Such Thing as Moving On." Filmed May 5, 2017 in Adelphi University, New York, TED video, 4:32. https://www.youtube.com/watch?v=kYWlCGbbDGI.

Psychology Today. "Toxic Positivity: Don't Always Look on the Bright Side." Accessed December 31, 2020. https://www.psychologytoday.com/us/blog/the-man-cave/201908/toxic-positivity-dont-always-look-the-bright-side.

CHAPTER 5

Feintuch, Stacy. "December is Hard." *Widow Wears Pink* (blog). *Living the Second Act*, December 11, 2016. https://livingthesecondact.com/2016/12/11/december-is-hard/.

Steinke-Baumgard, Michelle. "The Christmas Letter." *One Fit Widow* (blog). December 16, 2019. https://onefitwidow.com/the-christmas-letter/.

Steinke-Baumgard, Michelle. "Uncluttering our Christmas." *One Fit Widow* (blog). December 11, 2019. https://onefitwidow.com/no-more-clutter-for-christmas/.

Tischler, Mary Kate. "'Time Heals All Wounds:' I Call Bullshit!" *The Badass Widow* (blog). March 30, 2018. https://badasswidow.wordpress.com/?fbclid=IwAR2Mm4RnbWqTUC8HTZqJ7te-23ORZjdtVj8_O7lUc6BKloWmv1nFcFC__MTs.

Weiss, Debbie. "Coping with Widowhood over the Holidays." *The Hungover Widow* (blog). November 21, 2016. https://www.the-hungoverwidow.com/widowed-over-the-holidays/.

CHAPTER 6

Fivecoat-Campbell, Kerri. "How to Get Through the Fog of Grief." *NextAvenue*, May 7, 2019. https://www.nextavenue.org/fog-of-grief/.

Lewis, C.S. *A Grief Observed*. Read by Douglas Gresham. Harper Collins, 2014. Audible audio ed., 1hr., 53min.

Nash, Robert. "Are Memories Reliable?" *The Conversation*, December 17, 2018. https://www.google.com/amp/s/theconversation.com/amp/are-memories-reliable-expert-explains-how-they-change-more-than-we-realise-106461.

Schulman, Lisa. "Before and After Loss: A Neurologist's Perspective on Loss, Grief and the Brain." *JHU Press Blog* (blog). December 12, 2018. https://www.press.jhu.edu/news/blog/and-after-loss-neurologist%E2%80%99s-perspective-loss-grief-and-brain.

Steinke-Baumgard, Michelle. *Healthy Healing: A Guide to Working Out Grief.* New York: Harper-Collins, 2017.

Vasquez, Alejandra. "What Does it Mean to Have 'Widow Brain' After a Spouse Dies." *Cake*, December 15, 2020. https://www.joincake.com/blog/widow-brain/.

CHAPTER 7

Brown, Brené. Interview by Oprah Winfrey. *Super Soul Sunday.* Oprah Winfrey Network, March 17, 2013. https://www.youtube.com/watch?v=RKV0BWSPfOw.

Carandang, Carlo. "How Being Widowed Affects Your Anxiety." *Anxiety Boss*, July 18, 2014. https://anxietyboss.com/how-being-widowed-affects-your-anxiety/.

CBC. "Widowhood Can Shorten a Partner's Lifespan." Accessed January 4, 2021. https://www.google.com/amp/s/www.cbc.ca/amp/1.1125407.

Kübler-Ross, Elisabeth, and David Kessler. *On Grief and Grieving: Finding the Meaning of Grief Through the Five Stages of Loss.* New York: Scribner, 2005.

Sine, Richard. "Beyond 'White Coat Syndrome.'" *WebMD*, July 31, 2008. https://www.webmd.com/anxiety-panic/features/beyond-white-coat-syndrome#1.

Steinke-Baumgard, Michelle. "The Christmas Letter." *One Fit Widow* (blog). December 16, 2019. https://onefitwidow.com/the-christmas-letter/.

CHAPTER 8

Sandberg, Sheryl, and Adam Grant. *Option B: Facing Adversity, Building Resilience, and Finding Joy.* New York: Alfred A. Knopf, 2017.

CHAPTER 9

Daniher, Neale. "Fight MND." Melbourne Football Club. Streamed live on June 5, 2019. YouTube video, 1:25. https://www.youtube.com/watch?v=8H_aAmL-1NI&feature=emb_logo.

Funeral Service Foundation. *Youth and Funerals: Understanding the Important Role Funerals and Memorialization Play in the Lives of Youth.* Wisconsin: Funeral Service Foundation, 2020. https://indd.adobe.com/view/3336b310-bd79-47b1-a48e-f4d68f865124.

Hospice Foundation of America. "Children & Grief." Accessed January 6, 2021. https://hospicefoundation.org/Grief-(1)/Children-and-Grief.

Owens, Darrell. "Recognizing the Needs of Bereaved Children in Palliative Care." *Journal of Hospice & Palliative Care.* Volume 10, Issue 1 (January-February 2008): 14-16. https://journals.lww.com/jhpn/Citation/2008/01000/Recognizing_the_Needs_of_Bereaved_Children_in.6.aspx.

CHAPTER 10

Good Grief. "Compassion. Support. Community." Accessed January 8, 2021. https://good-grief.org/.

The National Alliance for Grieving Children. "About Childhood Grief." Accessed January 8, 2021. https://childrengrieve.org/resources/about-childhood-grief.

CHAPTER 11

Feintuch, Stacy. "The Worst Days Were During a Power Outage." *Widow Wears Pink* (blog). July 26, 2016. https://livingthesecondact.com/2016/07/26/the-blackout/.

Feintuch, Stacy. "When my Daughter Went Dark." *Widow Wears Pink* (blog). August 18, 2016. https://livingthesecondact.com/2016/08/18/amandas-story/.

Kessler, David. *Finding Meaning: The Sixth Stage of Grief.* New York: Scribner, 2019.

Kübler-Ross, Elisabeth, and David Kessler. *On Grief and Grieving: Finding the Meaning of Grief Through the Five Stages of Loss.* New York: Scribner, 2005.

Young Widow (@byyoungwidow). "Kinda wanting this again...#Widowhood." Twitter. July 13, 2020, 5:04 p.m.

CHAPTER 12

Barnes, Cheryl. "#Grieving While Black." *Black Women Widows Empowered* (blog). June 11, 2020. https://www.blackwomenwidowsempowered.com/post/grievingwhileblack.

Barrett, Gena-mour. "Seven Things No One Tells You About Losing A Parent as A Child." *BuzzFeed*, March 16, 2020. https://

www.buzzfeed.com/genamourbarrett/things-no-one-tells-you-about-losing-a-parent-as-a-child.

Steinke-Baumgard, Michelle. "Brown-Eyed Boy." *HuffPost*, September 10, 2014. https://www.huffpost.com/entry/browneyed-boy_b_5563661.

Your Tango. "Twenty-Seven Quotes to Help You Heal After Losing a Child." Accessed February 11, 2021. https://www.yourtango.com/2017300748/20-quotes-help-you-heal-loss-child.

CHAPTER 13

Brown, Brené. "Don't Be Afraid to Fall." University of Texas at Austin. Streamed live on May 23, 2020. YouTube video, 2:00-13:34. https://news.utexas.edu/2020/05/23/dont-be-afraid-to-fall-brene-brown-delivers-message-of-resilience-for-2020-graduates/.

Gladwell, Malcolm. *David and Goliath: Underdogs, Misfits, and the Art of Battling Giants.* New York: Little, Brown and Company, 2013.

National Alliance for Grieving Children. "About Childhood Grief." Accessed January 16, 2021. https://childrengrieve.org/resources/about-childhood-grief.

CHAPTER 14

Doughty, Elizabeth A., Adriana Wissel, and Cynthia Glorfield. *Current Trends in Grief Counseling.* Paper based on a program presented at the 2011 American Counseling Association and Exposition, March 23-27, 2011. Alexandrea: Vistas Online, 2011. Accessed December 20, 2020.https://www.counseling.org/resources/library/vistas/2011-V-Online/Article_94.pdf.

Kessler, David. *Finding Meaning: The Sixth Stage of Grief.* New York: Scribner, 2019.

Kübler-Ross, Elisabeth, and David Kessler. *On Grief and Grieving: Finding the Meaning of Grief Through the Five Stages of Loss.* New York: Scribner, 2005.

Tischler, Mary Kate. "'Do you see the butterflies circling my head?" *The Badass Widow* (blog). January 24, 2019. https://badasswidow.wordpress.com/?fbclid=IwAR1M_DGhb-D8WYZ98c_f2ZlU5xGMX1ryFnh-PJ2jiTSpnYa2OlGziNHv-NOGQ.

TSOT. "Angel Number 89." Accessed January 17, 2021. https://thesecretofthetarot.com/angel-number-89/.

CHAPTER 15

Brown, Brené. Interview by Oprah Winfrey. *Super Soul Sunday.* Oprah Winfrey Network, March 17, 2013. https://www.youtube.com/watch?v=RKVoBWSPfOw.

Burger, Kevyn. "'Not a Single Casserole'—What It's Like to Be Widowed by COVID-19." *NextAvenue*, July 10, 2020. https://www.nextavenue.org/widowed-by-covid-19/.

Garman, Jennifer. *Flourish: 7 Ways Gratitude Can Transform Your Life.* Potomac: New Degree Press, 2020.

Kübler-Ross, Elisabeth, and David Kessler. *On Grief and Grieving: Finding the Meaning of Grief Through the Five Stages of Loss.* New York: Scribner, 2005.

Sandberg, Sheryl, and Adam Grant. *Option B: Facing Adversity, Building Resilience, and Finding Joy.* New York: Alfred A. Knopf, 2017.

Steinke-Baumgard, Michelle. "Say Their Name." *One Fit Widow,* November 18, 2018. https://onefitwidow.com/say-their-name/.

Waters, Brad. "The New 10 Traits of Emotionally Resilient People." *Psychology Today,* December 12, 2018. https://www.psychologytoday.com/us/blog/design-your-path/201812/the-new-10-traits-emotionally-resilient-people.

Weiss, Debbie. "Using a Beginner's Mind to Cope with the Loneliness of Widowhood." *The Hungover Widow* (blog). March 14, 2018. https://thehungoverwidow.com/loneliness-of-widowhood-adopting-a-beginners-mind/.

CHAPTER 16

Kessler, David. *Finding Meaning: The Sixth Stage of Grief.* New York: Scribner, 2019.

Pogosyan, Marianna. "In Helping Others, You Help Yourself." *Psychology Today,* May 30, 2018. https://www.psychologytoday.com/us/blog/between-cultures/201805/in-helping-others-you-help-yourself.

CHAPTER 17

Feldman, David. "The Power of Rituals to Heal Grief." *Psychology Today*, September 28, 2019. https://www.psychologytoday.com/us/blog/supersurvivors/201909/the-power-rituals-heal-grief.

Henes, Mama Donna. "Why We Need Rituals in Our Lives." *HuffPost*, May 17, 2013. https://www.huffpost.com/entry/rituals_b_3294412.

CHAPTER 18

Govender, Serusha. "Is Crying Good for You?" *WebMD*. Accessed February 11, 2021. https://www.webmd.com/balance/features/is-crying-good-for-you#1.

Harvard Health Publishing. "Sour Mood Getting You Down?" Accessed January 21, 2021. https://www.health.harvard.edu/mind-and-mood/sour-mood-getting-you-down-get-back-to-nature.

Nair, Lakshmy. "How Exercise Improves Mood." *Livestrong*, August 14, 2008. https://www.livestrong.com/article/530791-does-exercise-make-you-happy/.

Steinke-Baumgard, Michelle. "Healing from Trauma—Why You Shouldn't Leave Your Body Behind." *One Fit Widow* (blog), December 10, 2019. https://onefitwidow.com/healing-from-trauma-why-you-shouldnt-leave-the-body-behind/.

CHAPTER 19

Brown, Brené. *Gifts of Imperfection*. Minnesota: Hazelden, 2010.

Kessler, David. *Finding Meaning: The Sixth Stage of Grief.* New York: Scribner, 2019.

Lewis, C.S. *A Grief Observed.* Read by Douglas Gresham. Harper Collins, 2014. Audible audio ed., 1hr., 53min.

Luscombe, Belinda. "The Divorce Rate is Dropping: That May Not Actually Be Good News." *Time*, November 26, 2018. https://time.com/5434949/divorce-rate-children-marriage-benefits/.

Manson, Mark. "Fuck Yes or No." *Mark Manson: Life Advice that Doesn't Suck*, July 8, 2013. https://markmanson.net/fuck-yes.

Phillips, Kerry. "But You're with Someone New—Why the Grief?" *Young, Widowed & Dating* (blog), August 7, 2020. https://youngwidowedanddating.com/2020/08/07/why-the-grief/.

Shetty, Jay. "If You've Been Rejected—Watch This." October 16, 2018, YouTube video: 2:48-3:14. https://www.youtube.com/watch?v=I5ENsv_yqqQ.

Steinke-Baumgard, Michelle. "I May Be Remarried, But I'm Still a Widow." *HuffPost*, December 6, 2017. https://www.huffpost.com/entry/dear-widow-police-i-wont-_b_8234798.

CHAPTER 20

Brown, Brené. *Braving the Wilderness.* New York: Random House, 2017.

Kessler, David. *Finding Meaning: The Sixth Stage of Grief.* New York: Scribner, 2019.

Kübler-Ross, Elisabeth. *Death: The Final Stage of Growth.* New Jersey: Prentice-Hall, 1975.

Lewis, C.S. *A Grief Observed.* Read by Douglas Gresham. Harper Collins, 2014. Audible audio ed., 1hr., 53min.

Robinson, Katie. "The Secret Meaning of the Lotus Flower." *Town & Country,* August 12, 2020. https://www.townandcountrymag.com/leisure/arts-and-culture/a9550430/lotus-flower-meaning/.

Rosen, Michael. *Going on a Bear Hunt.* Massachusetts: Candlewick Press, 1997.